Picnic

125 Recipes with 29 Seasonal Menus

DeeDee Stovel

STOREY
BOOKS

Recipe credits

Recipe on page 176 from *101 Perfect Chocolate Chip Cookies* by Gwen Steege, Storey Books, 2000.

Recipe on page 62 from *Garden Way's Joy of Gardening Cookbook* by Janet Ballantyne, Garden Way, Inc., 1984.

Recipe on page 170 based on a recipe from *The Moosewood Cookbook* by Mollie Katzen, Ten Speed Press, 1977.

Recipe on page 103 reprinted by permission of the Junior League of Palo Alto, California, from *A Private Collection.*

Recipes on page 150, page 151, and page 175 printed by permission of the Oakville Grocery Co., Oakville, California.

Recipes on pages 152 and 153 printed by permission of the ABC Bakery in Napa, California.

All recipes in the "Baby, It's Cold Outside Picnic" reprinted by permission of Irene Maston, innkeeper/chef at Andrie Rose Inn, Ludlow, Vermont.

Recipes on pages 65 and 67–68 are printed by permission of Bobbi Crosby.

The mission of Storey Communications is to serve our customers by publishing practical information that encourages personal independence in harmony with the environment.

Edited by Sally Patterson, Marie Salter, and Dianne M. Cutillo
Copyedited by Arlene Bouras
Cover design by Meredith Maker
Cover photographs by © Polly Wreford/Homes & Gardens/IPC Syndication; © Stock Food America; © Index Stock
Text design by Lisa Hollander
Text production by Erin Lincourt
Line drawings on pages iv, 13, 41, 88, 115, and 155 by Carleen Powell
Indexed by Nan Badgett/Word•a•bil•i•ty

Printed in Canada by Transcontinental
10 9 8 7 6 5 4 3 2

Library of Congress Cataloging-in-Publication Data

Stovel, DeeDee.
    Picnic : 125 recipes with 29 seasonal menus / DeeDee Stovel.
       p. cm.
    ISBN 1-58017-377-2 (alk. paper)
    1. Outdoor cookery. 2. Picnicking. I. Title.

TX823 .S833 2001
641.5'78—dc21   00-067127

DEDICATION

To My Daughters,
Kate and Meg

CONTENTS

Summer Spreads

Autumn Outings

Winter Wanderings

PREFACE

The more cookbooks, novels, and magazines I read, the more I realize that people all over the world love to picnic, maintaining unique traditions for making and packing food to share with family and friends in the great outdoors. The picnics I grew up with were of the commonplace variety, mostly in our backyard or the neighbors' yards. But what I recall most fondly are the faces of dear people, the warmth of friendship, and the flavors of favorite recipes.

This book is sprinkled with family and friends who joined me in countless outdoor meals and adventures and who inspired or shared many of the recipes and menus in this book. It is my hope that this book will help you make many special picnic memories of your own. I hope the menus and recipes included here (those marked with an asterisk in the menus) will serve as a guide as you create your own picnic traditions.

A Favorite Picnic?

While writing this book, I asked many people to tell me about their favorite picnic. Invariably heads tilted back, eyes shut, and smiles crept across faces. Picnics nourish the body, mind, and soul.

One friend recalls a starlight picnic on a hill within walking distance of home after a long, hard week of work. The toils of the week melted under the soothing starlight. Another evening picnic with a romantic twist took place on a beach in the moonlight at Half Moon Bay in California.

I remember family picnics on a small bay in Rhode Island, where our friends ordered a huge clambake layered with clams at the bottom

and lobsters at the top. We usually skipped the middle layers of fish and vegetables.

My most unusual picnic was eaten on a bus crossing the desert. After a delightful week in Ogden, Utah, our hostess packed us a picnic lunch of antelope sandwiches on which we gratefully munched as we crossed the Great Salt Lake Desert and Nevada on the way to San Francisco. The possibilities are endless!

A Word about the Recipes

These are my favorite recipes, which contain my favorite foods. Some go back to my grandmother's youth, many have been collected along the way from friends and family, and others are the result of my own experimentation. If you enjoy fresh foods, a well-balanced diet, have a sweet tooth, and make an effort to cut down on the sugar, salt, and fat in your diet, you share my tastes. These recipes do not avoid the villains of the American diet, but the amounts are kept low in most recipes.

I rarely sift flour. If the recipe calls for sifted flour, be sure to sift *before* measuring, as the volume changes with sifting.

Generally, the recipes are for eight people. Cut the recipes in half if your outing will consist of a quartet, or plan to have leftovers. Romantic picnics for two are designed for smaller quantities.

The recipes also are a reflection of my having grown up on the East Coast and living in New England for many years. There is also a strong California connection based on one year of residence, many visits, and a growing fascination with the climate, land, and abundance of intriguing foods and recipes — thus, the bicoastal flavor of this book.

May good food, good friends, and happy moments make all of your picnics memorable!

ACKNOWLEDGMENTS

*G*athering people around good food in a lovely setting was what family meant to my mother, Beatrice McCoy. She was locally known as a good cook. Seemingly without effort, she produced wonderful meals for family and friends. Her admonition to never economize on food remains with me, even though I know it is possible to do so and still enjoy great food. We must all eat to live, but in my family the emphasis was on living to eat. My mother was an artist who loved to cook. Her artistry was expressed in the care with which she prepared food and the beauty of its presentation. I am grateful to her.

My husband, Jack, willingly was the chief sampler of picnic fare. My daughters, Kate and Meg, participated in many picnics, and also helped test and review recipes. Their help and encouragement were invaluable. And I must also say that I appreciate my friends and family who sampled recipes, commented on the food and menus, gave ideas for recipes, and joined us in memorable picnics.

Thanks also to Sally Patterson of Storey Books, who oversaw the revisions of *Picnic*, for her encouragement as well as her editorial and culinary skills. I also appreciate the fine editing skills of Arlene Bouras, Marie Salter, and Dianne Cutillo and the enthusiasm for this project of Maggie Lydic.

WHAT IS A PICNIC?

A picnic evokes thoughts of leisure, relaxation, and enjoyment of the outdoors. It can be a still life in the open air or a boisterous frolic on the beach. Some picnics celebrate a special occasion, some offer the opportunity for friends to gather, and others provide an excuse for breaking the routine of daily life. In all cases, food is the centerpiece. Ask friends to go on a picnic with you and watch their eyes light up. A picnic is more than eating a meal, it is a pleasurable state of mind. "Let's go on a picnic" means "Let's have fun."

The people, the place, and the food are the essential ingredients of a memorable picnic. A truly magnificent picnic consists of dear friends or family, a spectacular setting, and delectable food and drink. You choose the companions and the site, and this book will provide you with recipes and ideas for the food and its presentation.

Picnics in Art

The history of picnics and eating outdoors is visually evident when one strolls through a museum of European paintings. Recall the images of great outdoor eating and drinking extravaganzas among the peasants in Peter Brueghel's works. The Impressionists, particularly Claude Monet and Edouard Manet, were fond of depicting romantic meals in secluded gardens. The most striking and well-known impressionist picnic painting is Manet's *Le Déjeuner sur l'herbe* ("Picnic on the Grass"), where the food clearly was not the main focus of the afternoon. Dining outdoors evokes festivity and romance, even though, in some cases, it is dictated by the necessity of cooking out-of-doors.

Picnics in History

Historically, picnics were meals to which each person attending contributed something. This idea of a "potluck" meal goes back to the Greek word *syncomist*, which means "brought from different places and put together." A syncomist initially was a coarse bread made of the by-products of flour. *Syncomist* was expanded to designate a meal in common to which everyone brings something, or a picnic.

These communal meals spread throughout the continent and were enjoyed by Scandinavians, Germans, and French. The picnic as an English institution was first described in the early 19th century as a fashionable social entertainment to which everyone took something. The institution evolved to include excursion parties to the country, where either everyone contributed food or one person provided the entire picnic. In the early 19th century, the English had a Picnic Society devoted to entertainment and theatricals as well as dining, where each member contributed something. The English, French, and other Europeans continue this tradition of outdoor dining.

Picnic Entertaining

Picnics are the ultimate in do-ahead entertaining. Whether served at a fabulous outdoor spot, in the backyard, or at the dining room table, all the food is prepared and stored in containers that will keep it safe, appetizing, and ready to serve at the desired temperature. The cook does not have to deal with the last-minute panic of wondering if all the dishes will be ready at the same time and at the right temperature. All the hostess has to do is put it out and enjoy the party.

> *eating themselves on the green sward they eat while the corks fly and there is talk, laughter and merriment, and perfect freedom, for the universe is their drawing room and the sun their lamp. Besides, they have appetite, nature's special gift, which lends to such a meal a vivacity unknown indoors, however beautiful the surroundings.*
>
> — French gastronome Brillat-Savarin

The Sandwich Story

Our present-day concept of a sandwich is often associated with portable meals or picnics. The idea of a sandwich as a snack goes back to Roman times. Scandinavians perfected the technique with the Danish open-faced sandwich, or smorrebrod, consisting of thinly sliced, buttered bread and many delectable toppings. These elaborate concoctions are not as portable as their sturdy American counterparts but can be constructed on-site and are highly suitable for an elegant picnic. The Earl of Sandwich, John Montagu, the 18th-century gambler who was known to have sat at the gaming table for 24 hours with nothing more than roast beef placed between two slices of toast for his nourishment, is the person to whom we are indebted for putting a top on the sandwich.

PICNIC
PLANNING

What differentiates a picnic from other meals is that it's packed to go. Because the food must travel and the weather may be warm, the packing of the food and accoutrements becomes critical. This chapter provides you with some ideas and a checklist to simplify your picnic planning.

Modern technology has broadened the selection of picnic paraphernalia, with insulated bags, backpacks, and water bottles or wine duffels now widely available. There are compact sets for a simple bread, cheese, and wine picnic with corkscrew, cutting board, and knives, with or without an insulated duffel for the bottle of wine. At the other extreme are elaborate backpacks or totes completely outfitted with everything one could possibly need on a picnic. The advantage of a backpack is its comfort. Carrying picnic accoutrements on your back is easier than lugging a heavy basket, no matter how artfully arranged. Whatever your choice of carrier, I recommend leaving it packed with all but the food and ready to go.

Packing to Go

The perfect picnic basket contains all the things you will need to create an idyllic afternoon, evening, or morning with your friends in a beautiful spot. Perfection can be achieved in many ways and planning ahead can help, but don't plan so much that you lose the sense of spontaneity that is essential to a picnic. Since you have to carry the basket, you don't want to take everything you could possibly ever need, you want the things that will make this event memorable and fun. There are different baskets for different types of picnics. Everyone has a different image of perfection, but let me share mine with you.

My favorite picnic image is of an antique market basket with a loose bouquet of fresh flowers poking out of one corner, a bottle of wine protruding from another, a fresh tablecloth covering fresh loaves of bread, garden vegetables converted to savory servings, chilled meats and cheeses, a luscious dessert, and steaming coffee. I like a cloth tablecloth and napkins and, depending on the occasion, enjoy colorful paper and plastic products for plates and tableware. For elegant picnics, I'd choose glassware, china, and silverware unless a hike is involved.

I personally like baskets of all sorts and shapes and am a sucker for them at antiques and secondhand stores. If you prefer new items, today you can find extremely well-equipped picnic baskets with matching plates and utensils, cloth napkins and tablecloth, stemware, and containers for the food. These traditional wicker baskets are often lined in gingham. If your tastes are less traditional, insulated bags, coolers, duffels, and cloth totes can serve as the "perfect picnic basket." Whatever you choose, pack your basket with as much food, drink, and excitement as it will hold.

Keeping Food Safe

At the end of the following recipes, you will find special packing tips. Safety is the main issue. Preventing bacterial growth that could cause illness can be accomplished by observing some simple procedures. Because picnic food often sits for long periods of time without direct heat or conventional refrigeration, observing sanitary practices in preparation and storage becomes particularly important. Clean hands and work surfaces are basic and essential. Keeping fresh foods in the refrigerator before and after preparation is essential. Using vinegars, lemon juice, and acidic ingredients in recipes is a useful way to avoid bacterial growth. Keeping cold foods cold and hot foods hot is the goal for both safety and appeal.

Keeping Food Cold

Preparing foods that will be served cold is the least complicated approach. Foods can be prepared, placed in traveling containers, and refrigerated or frozen until it's time to pack the picnic basket. The problem of soggy sandwiches can be eliminated by wrapping the bread in a plastic bag and packing the filling ingredients separately, then chilling them in the cooler. All cold food should be refrigerated until it is *thoroughly* cold. Meat, poultry, or fish that is to be grilled can be carried frozen to the picnic in the cooler and slowly thawed en route. Do not let meats, poultry, or fish thaw at room or air temperature, because bacteria can form on the warm outer surfaces. Cold food can be packed in cold thermos bottles, stowed in coolers with ice or freezer packs, or wrapped in heavy tablecloths, quilts, or layers of newspaper and placed in the picnic basket with a chunk of ice.

REMEMBER THE ENVIRONMENT

Care for the land on which you have your picnic and abide by the backcountry rule that you leave nothing but your footprints. Avoid excess use of disposable plastics and foam cups and plates. Take a garbage bag and collect all your trash and take it home, or leave it in an appropriate roadside trash container. See how little trash you can generate on your picnic. There are many beautiful, colorful throwaway picnic items on the market, including plates, cups, and napkins. There are also attractive lasting ones. If you plan to picnic frequently, it will benefit both you and the environment to invest in some permanent picnicware.

On our family camping trips, we created chunks of ice by thoroughly cleaning half-gallon cardboard milk containers, filling them almost to the top with water, and freezing them the night before we left. The chunk of ice lasted about a day, and the meltwater provided a refreshing drink for tired, thirsty campers. You can see the necessity of cleaning the container first. Plan to take your own water supply, as even the most sparkling streams may be polluted with animal bacteria or chemical waste. In hot weather, if people will be exercising, sufficient amounts of water are essential.

Keeping Food Hot

Packing food that should be served hot is more of a challenge. For liquids, bring the food to as high a temperature as you can and then put it into a thermos bottle that you have just rinsed with boiling water. For other foods, also bring them to a high temperature and then wrap them in heavy-duty aluminum foil and place them in an insulated bag or a heavy cloth. If you can keep the food above 140°F, it should be quite safe. For winter picnics at subfreezing temperatures, this can be difficult. I recommend bringing hot drinks and/or soups in a good-quality thermos and not attempting to keep other foods hot on a cold day. With hot foods, it is best not to take home leftovers. For cold foods, leftovers can be packed in the cooler for not more than four hours. Remember the old adage "When in doubt, throw it out." Eat all you take, but take plenty of food, because fresh air enhances the appetite. Plan well and cook well and there won't be many leftovers.

What to Take to Create Ambience

Besides carefully chosen and prepared food, a picnic includes the plates, the flatware, colorful napkins, tablecloths, and cups. Essentials include matches and garbage bags. Special touches are fresh flowers, mints, and candles. Don't forget a corkscrew if you bring wine. To avoid forgetting an essential item, a checklist is helpful, and a prepacked picnic basket is even better, because then you can be spontaneous and just grab your basket and go. With all these notes on preparation, remember that a picnic is fun. Don't get so overburdened with the planning that you don't want to bother with the picnic. Do it in a way that suits your style and inclination. Create a perfect day by combining good company and good food in a beautiful setting.

A Taste of the Past

For a slightly different approach, or for a Victorian picnic, you might refer to Mrs. Beeton's Book of Household Management, *in which she lists "Things not to be forgotten at a picnic." Our idea of essentials is somewhat different from Mrs. Beeton's in 1859:*

A stick of horseradish, a bottle of mint-sauce well corked, a bottle of salad dressing, a bottle of vinegar, made mustard, pepper, salt, good oil, and pounded sugar. If it can be managed, take a little ice. It is scarcely necessary to say that plates, tumblers, wine-glasses, knives, forks, and spoons must not be forgotten; as also teacups and saucers, 3 or 4 teapots, some lump sugar, and milk, if this last-named article cannot be obtained in the neighborhood. Take 3 corkscrews.

Baskets at the Ready

Some people choose to have their basket ready to travel so they can move at the hint of a picnic. Those people also have on hand a selection of ground covers, including reed mats, space blankets, beach towels, blankets, and quilts.

Essentials

These are the basics. You may well want to keep these items stocked in your picnic basket and ready to go.

- ❏ Plates
- ❏ Tableware
- ❏ Glassware
- ❏ Cutting board and knife
- ❏ Ground cloth, blankets, old quilts, or whatever suits your mood
- ❏ Paper napkins
- ❏ Tablecloth
- ❏ Corkscrew (for those who like wine)
- ❏ Bottle opener (for those who don't)
- ❏ Paper towels or wipes
- ❏ Garbage bags
- ❏ Insect repellent
- ❏ Sunscreen

Nonessential but Nice

These items depend on your mood and style:

- ❏ Candles, candle holders, and matches
- ❏ Flowers and vase
- ❏ Wineglasses
- ❏ China, crystal, and silverware
- ❏ Cloth napkins or bandanas
- ❏ Rattan or paper fans
- ❏ Umbrella, sunshade, or hats
- ❏ Flashlight

Rainy-Day Alternatives

We envision glorious, sunny weather for our picnics, and unless we live in a perpetually sunny climate, we cannot count on that. When the weather doesn't cooperate with our plans, we have several options: We can cancel our picnic, we can reschedule it, or we can choose another location under cover. In choosing the third alternative, some of our picnics may end up on the dining room table. That may result in a lovely picnic, but with some advance work, an even better site can be selected.

One of my favorite picnics is to gather family and friends several hours before sunset and hike a short distance up the Appalachian Trail to a beautiful meadow with a panoramic view of the mountains. In this mellow setting, we can watch the kaleidoscopic sky as the sun drops into the hills. On one such occasion, the weather was threatening. It was essential to find a place with a view. We located an unused building with a wide porch on the local college campus and were prepared for our picnic adventure in the event of a storm. In this case, the weather cleared just as we left and we were able to see the sunset after all.

A porch provides a welcome spot for a rainy-day picnic, because there is still some sense of being outdoors. On cold days, a picnic by the fire in the living room offers coziness with a relaxed atmosphere. Sunshine and picnics go together, but watching a rainstorm from a dry porch can offer a different way to enjoy the outdoors. In planning a picnic, be aware of the weather forecasts, but be resourceful! Think of ways to enjoy your picnic in all kinds of weather.

SPRING FLINGS

There is little sweeter than the first gentle breezes of spring. The crocuses start peeking out, a green haze covers the willows, tiny spears of green poke through the tangle of grasses and twigs in gardens and woodlands, and streams, unlocked from blankets of ice, gurgle happily down mountainsides. People slough off winter coziness and eagerly take to the outdoors. Any excuse will do to get outside, whether it is for a walk or a spring cleanup project, or — best of all — to have a picnic!

Picnics

SPRING DAY-HIKE PICNIC

SPRING BREAKFAST
AT THE BEACH PICNIC

"AFTER THE WEDDING"
BRUNCH PICNIC

SPRINGTIME AT THE OFFICE
LUNCH PICNIC

BREAKFAST IN A
MEADOW PICNIC

SPRING PROJECT PICNIC

Spring Day-Hike Picnic

Menu

Grilled chicken fillets*
in a spinach wrap

———

Artichoke salad*

———

Carrot sticks

———

Gingerbread* and fruit

———

Herbal iced tea*

*Recipe included in this chapter

Tiny, early spring violets, wild lily of the valley, and bunchberry poke their blossoms through the dense leaf cover along the trail and, with luck, a trillium or lady's slipper appears beneath the trees. Find yourself a glade of these miniature beauties and look through the leafless trees to find a view that would be hidden in the summer. It's often too muddy to hike in the spring and the bugs can be a bother, but it's a thrill to see things growing after a long winter. Pick a sunny day with soft, balmy breezes and enjoy the chance to dine in the open air.

What Else to Take

For the Food

- Thermos bottles
- Small insulated bag with ice pack
- Backpacks
- Water bottles

Extras

- Insect repellent
- Space blanket or moisture-resistant ground cloth

Grilled Chicken Fillets
in a Spinach Wrap

The simple satay marinade on this chicken is a staple in my kitchen. Not only is it fantastic on chicken, but I love it on grilled fish such as swordfish, halibut, or tuna. With or without the spinach wraps, this chicken is delicious.

---

8 *chicken breast halves, boned and skinned*

8 *spinach wraps or flour tortillas*

corn oil for cooking

MARINADE

½ *cup soy sauce*

¼ *cup mirin (sweet cooking sake)†*

2 *tablespoons lime juice*

2 *tablespoons sesame oil*

2 *large cloves of garlic, minced*

1 *tablespoon honey*

1 *tablespoon peeled and grated fresh ginger root*

½ *teaspoon Chinese five spice powder†*

†Available in natural foods stores

1. Rinse and pat dry the chicken; place in a shallow glass pan.
2. TO MAKE THE MARINADE, combine the marinade ingredients in a small bowl and pour over the chicken. Let sit for 30 minutes in the refrigerator.
3. Preheat gas grill to high.
4. Remove the chicken from the marinade and brush lightly with corn oil. Grill the chicken for 3 minutes on a side or until cooked through, brushing often with the marinade. An alternate cooking method is to cook on a ridged grill pan on the stovetop. Use medium-high heat with the exhaust fan running. Cook about 2 minutes per side until marked and cooked through. The trick is not to overcook the chicken and dry it out.
5. Let the chicken cool slightly and then refrigerate. Wrap the cold chicken in aluminum foil for transporting. Place the spinach wraps in a resealable plastic bag and pack them in your backpack. At the picnic site, roll the chicken in the spinach wraps, and enjoy hearty sandwiches of tender and moist grilled chicken.

Serves 8

Soft deli rolls or hamburger rolls are nice with this chicken. For a more substantial and tasty bread, try focaccia, lavash, or sourdough or Portuguese rolls.

Artichoke Salad

Jytte, a Danish friend, shared this recipe with me years ago. It quickly became a favorite item in picnics I catered for people attending the music festival at Tanglewood in Lenox, Massachusetts — summer home of the Boston Symphony Orchestra.

---

three 6-ounce jars marinated artichoke hearts with marinade

½ pound fresh mushrooms, washed, dried, and sliced

6 sun-dried tomatoes, cut into strips

4 scallions, thinly sliced, including some green tops

1 medium tomato, seeded and cut into bite-size chunks

1 stalk of celery, sliced

1 small sweet onion, thinly sliced

DRESSING

2 tablespoons balsamic vinegar

2 tablespoons olive oil

2 tablespoons vegetable oil

1 teaspoon lemon juice

1 teaspoon sugar

½ teaspoon dried oregano

¼ teaspoon salt

freshly ground black pepper

1. In a large bowl, combine all of the vegetables.

2. TO MAKE THE DRESSING, whisk the ingredients together in a small bowl and pour over the vegetables.

3. Let the salad sit in the refrigerator 8 hours or overnight. Place in a covered plastic dish and tuck it into your knapsack.

Serves 8

Late summer is artichoke season on the central California coast. Buy a bag of tiny artichokes, trim the ends off each leaf, cut in half lengthwise, and steam them to use in this salad. They are so small that the chokes usually don't have to be removed.

Gingerbread

Gingerbread is a classic spice cake that speaks of home and hearth. It's also a great traveling food because it's both sturdy and moist. It will keep for several days and freezes well. Enjoy it with whipped cream or brandied hard sauce, or have it plain.

---

1 cup molasses

½ cup buttermilk

1 egg, lightly beaten

2 cups all-purpose flour

½ cup sugar

1 teaspoon baking soda

½ teaspoon salt

1 teaspoon ground allspice

1 teaspoon ground cinnamon

1 teaspoon ground ginger

½ cup (1 stick) butter, melted

1 cup heavy cream, whipped (optional)

1. Preheat oven to 350°F. Grease a 9-inch square disposable baking pan.

2. In a small bowl, combine the molasses, buttermilk, and egg and stir to blend.

3. Sift the dry ingredients into a large bowl. Add the molasses mixture and mix well. Add the butter and stir just until blended.

4. Pour the batter into the prepared pan. Bake for 25 to 35 minutes, or until a tester inserted into the center comes out clean. Cool in the pan on a wire rack. When completely cool, cut into eight generous pieces and cover securely with aluminum foil for packing.

5. Put the whipped cream in a small covered container in the refrigerator until packing time. Wrap the container in heavy aluminum foil and place it in the pack. Stir before serving. If the hike is longer than 1½ hours, leave the whipped cream at home.

For a more intense ginger experience, substitute 1–2 tablespoons peeled and grated fresh ginger root for the 1 teaspoon ground ginger. Add it to the molasses mixture instead of to the dry ingredients.

Serves 8

Herbal Iced Tea

This cold infusion is refreshing on a warm spring day or in the heat of midsummer. It is a favorite with children, too.

6 bags of Orange Zinger, or other herbal tea

2 quarts cold water

2 tablespoons honey (optional)

lemon slices

1. Put the tea bags into a large pitcher.

2. Pour the water over the bags and add the honey, if desired. Store the pitcher in the refrigerator for at least 1 hour, during which time the tea will infuse the water.

3. Remove the tea bags and pour the cold tea into thermos bottles when ready for your hike. Put the lemon slices in a resealable plastic bag and serve them with the cups of tea for a refreshing drink after a long hike.

Makes 2 quarts

If time allows, make the tea in the traditional way by boiling water and pouring it over the tea bags. Steep for 5 minutes, and then store in the refrigerator.

Spring Breakfast at the Beach Picnic

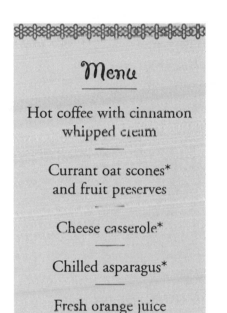

For those who love the ocean and are lucky enough to live near it, a warm spring weekend is a call to the sea. Begin a glorious day with breakfast or brunch on the beach. Fresh air, open space, and the sound and smell of the sea make a picnic on the beach one of the most perfect picnics. (If it is a gusty spring day, take along a kite for after-breakfast excitement.) A lakeside beach would be an equally nice way to celebrate the beginning of spring.

What Else to Take

For the Food

- A thermos
- A cooler
- Butter and a selection of fruit preserves in a small basket
- Mugs for coffee

Extras

- Beach blankets or towels
- Beach chairs
- Beach toys
- A kite
- Garbage bag

Special Note

Take a garbage bag and clean up everything. Remember, also, that what people throw overboard on boats ends up on somebody's beach. A trashy beach takes away the romance from the perfect picnic.

Currant Oat Scones

A cup of steaming coffee and a fresh scone is a glorious way to greet the day while sitting by the sea. While I recommend eating these fresh, they also freeze amazingly well.

1½ cups all-purpose flour

¾ cup old-fashioned rolled oats

¼ cup sugar

1 tablespoon baking powder

¼ teaspoon salt

4 tablespoons very cold butter, cut into chunks

2 eggs, well beaten

¼ cup heavy cream

½ cup currants

sweet butter and fruit preserves to serve with the scones

1. Preheat oven to 400°F.

2. Place the flour, oats, sugar, baking powder, and salt in a food processor. Process briefly. With the motor running, add the butter and process until the mixture resembles coarse crumbs.

3. Mix the eggs and cream in a small bowl. With the motor running, add the egg mixture to the flour mixture. Process until the dough forms a ball.

4. On a lightly floured surface, knead the currants into the dough until they are evenly distributed. Pat the dough into a circle approximately 6 to 8 inches in diameter and 1 inch thick.

5. Cut the circle in half and cut each half into six wedge-shaped pieces. Place the scones on an ungreased baking sheet. Bake for 15 minutes, or until golden brown. Wrap them in a fresh cloth napkin, place in a small basket, and hope that they are still warm when you get to the beach. Serve them with the butter and preserves.

Makes 12 scones

• *Traditional Scottish scones were originally made of oats and baked on a griddle. While our waistlines may not approve, the secret to our lighter, modern version is butter. Don't skimp in this recipe.*

• *Make two smaller circles for miniscones.*

• *Dried cranberries or chopped apricots are a lovely substitute for currants. Grated Cheddar cheese and half the sugar give a more savory scone.*

Cheese Casserole

My dear Aunt Edie passed this mouthwatering strata to me as one of her favorite brunch dishes. It is essentially a portable soufflé. Because of the bread, it will not completely deflate as it cools.

9 slices whole-wheat bread, cut into thirds

1 medium onion, chopped

1 pound Cheddar cheese, grated

4 eggs, lightly beaten

3 cups milk

1 tablespoon Worcestershire sauce

1 teaspoon dry mustard

½ teaspoon salt

¼ teaspoon white pepper

dash cayenne pepper

1. In a greased 2-quart casserole, place nine pieces of the bread. Sprinkle with one-third of the onion and one-third of the Cheddar. Repeat this layering until all of these ingredients are used.

2. In a 1-quart measuring cup, whisk together the eggs, milk, Worcestershire sauce, mustard, salt, pepper, and cayenne. Pour over the bread, onions, and Cheddar. Cover the casserole with plastic wrap and store in the refrigerator overnight.

3. Remove the casserole from the refrigerator 30 minutes before baking.

4. Preheat oven to 325°F.

5. Bake the casserole for 50 to 60 minutes. The casserole will be puffy as it comes out of the oven. It will deflate slightly as it cools, but the flavor will remain the same. Wrap the casserole in a towel to keep it warm when you take it to the beach.

Serves 8

Chilled Asparagus

*What says spring louder than fresh asparagus? The appearance
of these knobby spears heralds the season's warm, soft breezes.*

———————

2   *pounds fresh spring
    asparagus, washed and
    trimmed*
¼   *cup Lemon Butter (see
    page 143)*

1. Steam the asparagus for about 15 minutes or until tender crisp.

2. Spread the asparagus stems out in a low, flat dish.

3. Cover the bowl and chill for 1 hour. Drizzle tips with lemon butter before packing it in the basket.

Serves 8

Sangria

*My brother Dennis, who lived in Spain for three years, concocted this recipe
and considers it most like what he found in Madrid. I like to serve it in clear glass
pitchers because the color is so festive. A traditional pottery jug is also nice.*

———————

1 to 1.5 liters red wine
    one *1-liter Tom Collins mix*
      2 *cups Triple Sec*
      2 *ounces brandy*
      2 *apples, cored and thinly
        sliced*
      1 *orange, thinly sliced*
    lots of ice

1. Combine all ingredients except the ice.

2. Fill two large pitchers with ice and pour the sangria over the ice. Wrap the pitchers in blankets and transport to the beach.

Serves 8 to 12

"After the Wedding" Brunch Picnic

Weddings stretch from one-day events to wedding weekends to weeklong celebrations. A brunch for out-of-town guests on the morning after is almost as common as the rehearsal dinner. It gives the bride and groom, who usually attend, a chance to unwind and visit with their out-of-town friends in a relaxed way before the wedding is truly over. Remember to go light on the alcohol, as many guests have long drives ahead of them.

Wine Suggestions

Try an inexpensive Spanish sparkling wine, a good California champagne such as Korbel Brut or Extra Dry, or an Italian Prosecco.

Special Planning

A friend of the family or the family of the bride and groom is likely to plan this picnic. Because it takes place at someone's home, in a yard, or on a deck, the usual concerns about transporting foods are no longer an issue. Bouquets from the reception are all that is needed to set the stage for this festive occasion.

Zucchini and Sausage Pie

*T*his crustless quiche combines the savory taste of sausage with the sharpness
of cheese for an exceptional blend. For the piecrust-challenged, this recipe is
a welcome change. Cut the pie into small squares for a savory appetizer.

¼ cup vegetable oil
2 cups shredded zucchini
1 medium onion, chopped
½ pound bulk sausage
2 cups grated Swiss cheese
1 cup all-purpose flour
1 cup milk
½ cup half-and-half
2 tablespoons grated
    Parmesan cheese
2 eggs, lightly beaten
1 tablespoon butter, melted
½ teaspoon salt
½ teaspoon white pepper
dash ground nutmeg

1. Preheat oven to 400°F.

2. Heat the oil in a large skillet over medium heat and
sauté the zucchini and onion for 5 minutes, or until soft.
Remove from the pan and put into a large bowl. Add the
sausage to the skillet. Break up the sausage with a wooden
spoon and cook over medium heat until the pink color is
gone. Drain the sausage on paper towels.

3. Add the sausage to the zucchini and onion and mix.
Then add the remaining ingredients. Mix well and pour into
a 9-inch square baking pan. Bake for 40 minutes, or until a
knife inserted in the center comes out clean. Cool the pie in
the pan on a wire rack. Cut into squares and serve to the
guests.

Serves 8

Fresh Fruit Bowl Kaleidoscope

A large colorful bowl of fresh fruit is always welcome on my brunch table.
I like to use fruit that is in season because it is the freshest, juiciest, and tastiest.

---

3 *peaches, pitted and cut into 1-inch chunks*

2 *pounds watermelon, peeled, seeded, and cut into ½-inch cubes*

1 *pint strawberries, hulled and cut in half*

2 *nectarines, pitted and cut into 1-inch chunks*

1 *small cantaloupe, peeled, seeded and cut into ½-inch cubes*

1 *pint blueberries*

1 *cup green or red seedless grapes*

2 *tablespoons sugar*

¼ *cup Grand Marnier liqueur*

1 *cup raspberries*

DRESSING

1 *cup plain yogurt*

2 *tablespoons lemon juice*

2 *tablespoons sugar*

1. In a large bowl, mix the peaches, watermelon, strawberries, nectarines, cantaloupe, blueberries, grapes, and sugar. Pour the Grand Marnier over all and stir gently. Put the fruit into a glass serving bowl and sprinkle the raspberries over the top. Serve the fruit at room temperature.

2. TO MAKE THE DRESSING, combine the yogurt, lemon juice, and sugar in a small bowl. Serve in a pretty dish alongside the fruit bowl.

Serves 8

Use whatever combination of fruit looks best in the market. In-season fruits are the best and least expensive.

Tante's Coffee Cake

*My grandmother's sister, Tante Matilda (yes, I really had a
Great Aunt Tilly!), contributed this recipe to my mother's collection.
It was a regular at family parties and weekend breakfasts.*

---

4 tablespoons butter,
softened, plus 4 to 8
tablespoons melted
butter

¾ cup sugar

3 eggs

3 cups all-purpose
flour

1 tablespoon baking
powder

1 cup milk

1 teaspoon grated
lemon zest

¼ cup sugar mixed
with
1½ teaspoons
ground cinnamon

½ cup sliced
unblanched almonds

1. Preheat oven to 350°F. Grease two 9- by 13-inch baking pans.

2. In the large bowl of an electric mixer, cream the 4 tablespoons of softened butter and sugar until light and fluffy. Add the eggs and beat at medium speed until well blended.

3. Sift the flour and baking powder together in a medium-sized bowl. At low speed, alternately add the flour mixture and milk to the creamed mixture and continue beating until thick and light in color. Stir in the lemon zest until well mixed.

4. Spread the batter evenly into the prepared pans.

5. Spoon half of the melted butter over each cake and gently spread it with a spatula so it is evenly distributed. You don't want to mix it into the batter; you want to have a thin layer of melted butter over the top. (The layer will not be a smooth one.)

6. Sprinkle half of the cinnamon and sugar mixture over each cake, and then sprinkle half of the almonds over each cake.

7. Bake the cakes for 20 minutes, or until lightly browned around the edges. Cool the cakes in the pans on wire racks. Cut into 1½- by 3-inch rectangles and arrange on serving plates. Cover the plates with plastic wrap and store at room temperature until the picnic. The cakes can be made in advance and frozen.

Serves 32

Champagne Mimosas

A touch of champagne continues the festive atmosphere of the wedding. Diluting it with orange juice makes a refreshing morning drink. And, of course, I offer an equally attractive nonalcoholic beverage, which in this case is sparkling and fruity.

2 bottles champagne, chilled
2 cups chilled orange juice

1. For each glass of champagne, add ¼ cup of orange juice. Serve.

Serves 8

Fruit Punch

one 48-ounce bottle cranberry juice cocktail, chilled
one 1-liter bottle sparkling water, chilled
4 cups chilled pineapple juice
4 cups cold Red Zinger tea (use 6 tea bags)
1 ring of ice
1 orange, thinly sliced

1. Just before serving, pour all liquid ingredients into a punch bowl over the ice. Float the orange slices on top.

Serves 18 to 20

HOW TO MAKE A FRUITED OR FLOWERY ICE RING

Fill a ring mold halfway with tap or spring water. Place in freezer on a level shelf. Freeze until solid. Lay washed berries or pansies, Johnny-jump-ups, or other edible flowers on the ice. Cover with more water, and place in freezer on a level shelf. When ready to serve the punch, unmold the ice ring and place it upside down in the punch bowl. Fill the bowl with punch. Voilà!

Springtime at the Office Lunch Picnic

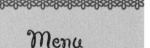

Menu

Fresh pea soup*

———

Thinly sliced turkey breast sandwiches on honey whole-wheat bread* with guacamole*

———

Bundt cake*

———

Chilled green grapes

———

Coffee, tea, or skim milk

*Recipe included in this chapter

"Make homemade cake and bread for my lunch? That's too much work," you might say to yourself. Baking does take time, which many devote only to holidays, if at all. However, here is a chance not only to provide some lunch treats for yourself and your family members, but to share some goodies with your fellow workers. In planning an office picnic to which everyone takes his or her own lunch, you can offer some delicious homemade cake or bread as a treat for all.

What Else to Take

• Brightly colored tablecloth
• Zany napkins

Beguiling Breads

Making homemade bread takes time and inclination but is worth the effort. This tasty and healthful whole-wheat bread is not dry or heavy. It freezes beautifully, when doubly wrapped. You are in charge of the bread you bake. For example, to lengthen a rising time, cover the bowl with plastic wrap and refrigerate overnight, until risen.

Fresh Pea Soup

Homemade soup may not seem to fit into a busy work schedule, but this taste of spring is quick, easy, and an absolute winner. My sister-in-law Susan introduced me to fresh pea soup, and I now welcome spring with at least one fresh batch.

2 cups shelled fresh peas
1 cup chicken stock (homemade, if available)
1 small onion, chopped
1 teaspoon butter
1 tablespoon lime juice
¼ teaspoon ground nutmeg
1 cup plain yogurt

1. Cook the peas in ¼ cup water in a microwave oven on High for 3 minutes or in a medium-sized saucepan for 5 to 6 minutes.

2. Heat the chicken stock in a microwave oven, then place it in a blender. Add the peas and cooking liquid and let the mixture sit for 5 minutes.

3. Meanwhile, sauté the onion in the butter for 3 minutes, or until soft. Add the onion mixture, lime juice, and nutmeg to the peas and purée until smooth.

4. Add the yogurt and blend briefly. Pour the soup into four 1-cup covered containers and chill until ready to pack one of them in your lunch bag.

Serves 4

• *I make this soup when peas are in season, because fresh peas are so fantastic. It's tasty enough with frozen, but incomparable with fresh peas.*

• *Smooth this soup out with cream instead of yogurt for a sublime result.*

Honey Whole-Wheat Bread

For years, my husband Jack supplied our family with loaves of this delicious, nutritious bread, a family favorite. He made four loaves at a time, and it was the only bread we ate. We used it for all kinds of sandwiches, for toast, and with bowls of hearty soup for a satisfying winter supper. I also loved grabbing a loaf to bring to a friend. When I taught home economics, many of my seventh-grade students learned to make this bread and were often amazed at how delicious a healthy bread can be.

2½ cups warm (110°F) water

2 tablespoons active dry yeast

⅓ cup powdered milk

¼ cup honey

3 tablespoons butter, softened

1 teaspoon salt

2½ cups all-purpose flour

4 to 5 cups whole-wheat flour

1. Place the water and yeast in a large bowl and let the mixture sit for 5 minutes until the yeast is dissolved.

2. Meanwhile, in a small bowl, mix the powdered milk, honey, butter, and salt into a paste. Add this to the yeast mixture and blend well with a large whisk.

3. Add the all-purpose flour and beat with the whisk or a wooden spoon until the flour is well blended. Gradually add the whole-wheat flour, 1 cup at a time, and continue beating with a wooden spoon. When the dough seems to come together in a ball in the center of the bowl and is soft but not sticky, scrape the sides of the bowl and dump the contents onto a lightly floured surface. At this point, you will not have added all the whole-wheat flour.

4. Knead the dough for about 10 minutes. As it gets sticky, add small amounts of the remaining whole-wheat flour. When the dough is well kneaded, it will have absorbed most of the flour and will be smooth and round and softly firm to the touch. It should not be sticky (too little flour) or rigid (too much flour).

5. Put the dough into a clean, oiled bowl; turn the dough over to coat it with oil; cover it with a damp cloth; and let it rise in a warm, draft-free place until it is double in bulk, about 45 minutes to 1 hour.

6. Grease two 9- by 4-inch loaf pans. When the dough has doubled in size, punch it down and knead it two times to form a smooth shape and to release the air bubbles. Divide the dough into two equal pieces and shape each one into a loaf. Place the loaves in the prepared pans and cover with a clean dish towel. Let the loaves rise for 1 hour or until again doubled in size.

7. While the dough is rising, preheat oven to 400°F. Bake the loaves for 40 to 50 minutes or until brown on top. Remove them from the pans immediately and cool on wire racks. When completely cool, store the loaves in plastic bags.

Makes 2 loaves

While it is tempting to taste bread when it is hot from the oven, you will find that it is much easier to slice when slightly cool. Storing bread in the refrigerator dries it out and speeds up the staling process. Bread that you will not eat within a few days is best stored in the freezer. You can quickly thaw it in a microwave oven.

Guacamole

Avocados and lime juice are the two essentials of guacamole, beyond which there are many variations. What follows is my never-fail recipe for basic guacamole.

1 ripe Hass avocado
1 medium tomato, chopped, with seeds and juice removed
2 tablespoons minced onion
1 teaspoon hot sauce
juice of 1 lime

1. Cut the avocado in half and remove the pit. Scoop out the flesh and place it in a medium-sized bowl. Mash the avocado with the back of a fork until it is smooth.

2. Add the tomato, onion, hot sauce, and lime juice to the avocado and mix well. Place the guacamole in a covered container and refrigerate until ready to use.

Makes 1 cup

Bundt Cake

*I love this Bundt cake for its rich, buttery flavor, hint of lemon,
and firm texture, which make it a great take-along dessert.
Because it is so rich and buttery, I recommend thin slices.*

1¾ cups sugar

1 cup (2 sticks) butter

1 cup plain yogurt

3 eggs

2 teaspoons grated lemon zest

1 teaspoon vanilla extract

2¼ cups all-purpose flour

½ teaspoon salt

½ teaspoon baking soda

1. Preheat oven to 325°F. Grease and lightly flour a Bundt pan.

2. In the large bowl of an electric mixer, cream together the sugar and butter until the mixture is light and fluffy. Add the yogurt, eggs, lemon zest, and vanilla. Continue beating until the mixture is well blended.

3. Sift the flour, salt, and baking soda into a medium-sized bowl and gradually add the flour mixture to the egg mixture with the mixer running at low speed. Beat the batter for 3 minutes, until light in color.

4. Pour the batter into the prepared pan and bake for 60 to 70 minutes or until lightly browned on top and a tester inserted in the cake comes out clean.

5. Cool upright on a wire rack for 15 minutes. Remove the cake from the pan and cool completely on a wire rack.

Serves 8

Butter Is Better

Be sure to use butter in this recipe. With a simple cake like this, butter is the flavor you want.

Breakfast in a Meadow Picnic

Menu

Fresh strawberries dipped
in confectioners' sugar

———

Country pâté* and
assorted crackers

———

Imported cheeses

———

Sunny morning muffins*
with sweet butter

———

Swiss chocolate
almond coffee

*Recipe included in this chapter

*I*magine it: A lovely lazy sunny morning with a pile of Sunday papers and delicious food to nibble on as the morning passes. Pack a beautiful basket of goodies that two of you can carry easily as you trudge to your meadow.

Wine Suggestions
Try a lighter French champagne such as Perrier-Jouët or a Crémant d'Alsace or a Spanish sparkling wine.

What Else to Take

- Blankets
- Beach chairs
- Sunscreen
- Sunday papers
- Books
- Visors or baseball caps

Flavored Coffees

*C*hoice overwhelms us, and in the realm of coffee it's no different. Among my favorites are hazelnut, Swiss chocolate almond, vanilla, and French roast. Experiment! You won't be sorry.

Country Pâté

This tasty pâté doesn't take long to make, but it requires some planning.
Cindy, a design director who loves to cook, gave me this recipe and I love it.

1¼ pounds chicken livers

6 tablespoons port wine

4 bay leaves, 2 crumbled and
  2 whole

dash dried thyme

4 slices imported ham

¾ pound bulk sausage

3 slices bread, soaked
  in ½ cup milk

½ cup dry white wine

1 clove of garlic, minced

freshly ground black pepper

6 slices bacon

1. Preheat oven to 375°F.

2. Rinse the chicken livers in cold water and pat dry. Place them in a bowl with the port, the 2 crumbled bay leaves, and thyme and marinate in the refrigerator for 2 hours.

3. Remove the bay leaves from the marinade and put three-quarters of the chicken livers and the marinade into a food processor. Reserve the remaining livers. Add the ham, sausage, and bread. Process until you have a coarse mixture. Stir in the wine, garlic, and pepper to taste.

4. Line an 8-inch square glass baking pan or a 9- by 5-inch glass loaf pan with 3 slices of the bacon. Spread half of the liver and sausage mixture in the pan. Add the reserved whole livers and cover with the remaining liver and sausage mixture. Top the pâté with the remaining bacon and the 2 whole bay leaves.

5. Cover the pan and place in a larger pan of boiling water — the water should come up the side of the pan 1½ to 2 inches — and bake for 1½ to 2 hours. Remove from the oven, pour off the juices, and place a weight on the pâté as it cools in the refrigerator. Wrap the cold pâté in plastic wrap and store in the refrigerator for 2 days before serving.

6. Slice enough for two and save the rest for a party.

Serves 8

Sunny Morning Muffins

*These muffins are so packed with goodies that they could be a meal in themselves.
They are my take on the famous Nantucket Morning Glory Muffins.*

1½ cups unbleached all-purpose flour

½ cup whole-wheat flour

¾ cup sugar

2 teaspoons baking soda

2 teaspoons ground cinnamon

½ teaspoon salt

3 eggs, lightly beaten

½ cup vegetable oil

2 cups grated carrots or zucchini, or a combination

½ cup coconut (optional)

½ cup chopped pecans

½ cup undrained crushed pineapple

½ cup golden raisins

1. Preheat oven to 350°F. Grease 15 muffin-pan cups.

2. Sift the two flours with the sugar, baking soda, cinnamon, and salt into a large bowl. In a small bowl, mix the eggs and oil and add to the flour mixture. Stir the batter just until the dry ingredients are moistened.

3. Fold the carrots, coconut, pecans, pineapple, and raisins into the batter and stir until blended.

4. Pour the batter into the prepared pans and bake for 25 to 30 minutes, or until a tester inserted into the center of a muffin comes out clean. Cool the muffins in the pans on a wire rack for 10 minutes. Remove the muffins from the pans and wrap four of them in a napkin. Put them into the picnic basket and hope that they will still be warm when you get to your meadow.

Makes 15 muffins

Store the rest of the muffins in the freezer after wrapping them in plastic wrap and placing them in a freezer bag. They will keep for several months.

Spring Project Picnic

*Recipe included in this chapter

When crocuses begin peeking their colorful heads through the soil and songbirds return to set up house, spring is on its way and it's time to get outdoors. I get excited about raking the lawn and any number of other springtime chores because they give me cause to be outside in the warm, fresh air.

For this picnic, assemble a group of vigorous, like-minded individuals and make a party out of a community service project. Plan to clean up a schoolyard or to plant a community garden. Organize the project and tools, and reward participants with a nice meal. Much of the menu can come from a deli, but to make this picnic special bring a few homemade items or ask your hard-working volunteers to contribute a specialty or two.

What Else to Take

- Tools for the cleanup project
- Garbage bags for hauling out the debris
- Paper tablecloth, plates, napkins, and cups
- Blankets for participants to sit on while they eat

Couscous

A staple of the North African diet, this Mediterranean dish is made from bits of semolina dough and is actually like a tiny pasta.

---

1 tablespoon olive oil
1 medium onion, thinly sliced
1 green bell pepper, chopped
1 red bell pepper, chopped
1 yellow bell pepper, chopped
2 cloves of garlic, minced
2 cups chicken broth
½ teaspoon salt
2 cups couscous
½ lemon, chopped
¼ teaspoon ground cumin
 freshly ground black pepper
 chopped spring chives

1. Add the olive oil to a medium saucepan and place pan over medium heat. Sauté onion for 2 minutes, until translucent. Add peppers and garlic and cook until tender crisp, about 5 minutes.

2. Stir in the broth and salt and bring to a boil over high heat. Add the couscous, lemon, cumin, and pepper to taste, stir and remove from heat. Cover and let sit for 5 minutes, or until liquid is absorbed. Fluff the grain and serve at room temperature; garnish with the chives. Place in a large covered plastic dish, and store in the refrigerator until ready to pack the picnic.

Serves 8

Add a simple vinaigrette to leftover couscous, or sprinkle with olive oil and balsamic vinegar. For a fantastic main course, add chunks of chicken.

Tender Spring Lettuce Salad
with Strawberries

*Early tender greens are a sure sign of spring. Strawberries
not only brighten the greens but add a special sweetness.*

---

6 cups mixed tender lettuce
leaves, washed, spun dry,
and torn into bite-sized
pieces

3 tablespoons extra virgin
olive oil

2 tablespoons balsamic
vinegar

freshly ground black pepper

1 pint fresh strawberries,
washed, hulled, and cut in
half if large

1 small red onion, thinly
sliced

½ cup toasted chopped
pecans†

¼ cup blue cheese, crumbled

†Toast the pecans for 5 to 10 minutes in
a toaster oven set at 400°F.

1. Just before leaving for the project, fill a large salad bowl with the lettuce. Spoon the olive oil over the lettuce and toss with salad servers. Repeat with vinegar. Grind pepper over the salad and toss again. Cover with plastic wrap and bring to project site.

2. Before serving, scatter the strawberries over the top, then the onion, the pecans, and finally the cheese over all. Toss lightly while serving.

Serves 8

Apricot Almond Bars

These sturdy bar cookies travel well. The delicate combination
of apricot and almond, however, is anything but sturdy.

---

1 cup dried apricots

½ cup water

½ cup (1 stick) unsalted
butter, softened

¼ cup granulated sugar

1 cup whole-wheat pastry
flour

⅓ cup plus 2 tablespoons
all-purpose flour

2 eggs

¾ cup firmly packed brown
sugar

¾ cup sliced unblanched
almonds

½ teaspoon almond extract

¼ teaspoon baking powder

1. Preheat oven to 350°F. Grease a 9-inch square pan.

2. In a small covered saucepan, bring the apricots and water to a boil. Turn off heat and let sit for 10 minutes, until apricots are plump. Drain and finely chop the apricots.

3. Meanwhile, cream together the butter, granulated sugar, whole-wheat flour, and the ⅓ cup all-purpose flour. Press into the prepared pan. Bake for 20 minutes, until lightly browned.

4. In a large bowl, combine the eggs, brown sugar, almonds, 2 tablespoons all-purpose flour, extract, and baking powder. Stir in the apricots. Spread the mixture on the crust. Bake for 20 to 25 minutes longer, until the top is set and browned around the edges.

5. Cool on a rack and cut into bars. Take to the picnic in an airtight tin.

Makes 16 bars

Whole-wheat pastry flour is one of my favorite ways to sneak nutrition into a delicacy. Unlike whole-wheat bread flour, this variety is low in gluten, the building block of bread, and therefore not a heavy flour. It adds nutrition and a nutty flavor but keeps pastries light.

SUMMER
SPREADS

Picnics fit my fantasy of what summertime should be: long sunny days, endless hours for enjoyment, and no stress or pressures. Despite the reality of a busy life, where such a fantasy is rarely realized, this idyll of summer persists in my mind. To recapture a bit of the dream of summer, plan a picnic on a beautiful day in a beautiful place. Take advantage of the long daylight hours and give yourself a break from pressures and "to do" lists. Gather a group to languidly celebrate the season with good food, fellowship, and fun.

Picnics

FAMILY CELEBRATION PICNIC IN THE BACKYARD	MUSIC FESTIVAL PICNIC
——	——
SUMMER CANOE PICNIC	CHAMPAGNE TEA PICNIC
——	——
BERRY-PICKING PICNIC	GARDEN PICNIC
——	——
NEIGHBORHOOD POOLSIDE PICNIC	SUNLIGHT THROUGH THE TREES PICNIC
——	——
SUMMER IN THE BERKSHIRES PICNIC	REUNION ON AN ISLAND PICNIC
——	——
SUMMER AT THE BEACH PICNIC	MOONLIGHT ON A MOUNTAINTOP PICNIC

Family Celebration Picnic in the Backyard

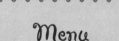

Menu

Taco salad*

Barbecued chicken*

Mixed bean salad*

Corn on the cob and
garden lettuce tossed salad

Gramma Bea's
strawberry shortcake*

Iced tea, cold beer, or
chilled white wine

*Recipe included in this chapter

Summer is often the time when families gather to share a vacation spot or a day together. When the clan gathers to celebrate a special occasion, everyone can contribute something to the meal. Depending on the size of your family, this could be either a small or a very large party. The recipes in this chapter are generally made to serve eight people. If you are serving a large crowd, have several people make the same dish or have them make a double batch.

Beer and Wine Suggestions

Try Anchor Steam Beer from San Francisco, Samuel Adams Beer, or Pilsner Urquel; for wine, Alsatian Pinot Blanc or California Sauvignon Blanc.

What Else to Take

- Bouquets of summer flowers in rustic containers and pots, arranged on tables and benches
- Balloons and streamers
- Croquet
- Badminton
- Paddleball

Taco Salad

This is called a salad but is really a hearty appetizer. In essence, it is a dip with several layers. Use your imagination to add more layers. It is best to prepare the parts ahead of time and assemble it just before serving.

---

one 15-ounce can refried beans (optional)

1½ cups grated Cheddar or Monterey Jack cheese (optional)

1 cup Guacamole (see recipe page 31)

½ cup medium salsa

½ cup plain yogurt

2 medium tomatoes, chopped and seeded

6 scallions, chopped, including at least 1 inch of the green tops

1 large bag nacho chips

1. In a 10-inch deep-dish nonmetal pie pan (preferably a decorative one), spread the beans evenly over the bottom. Sprinkle the cheese over the beans. Place in a microwave oven for 30 seconds on high, until the cheese melts.

2. Spread the guacamole over the cheese, then a thin layer of the salsa. Gently spread the yogurt over the salsa.

3. Arrange the tomatoes in a ring around the outer edge of the pie pan. Make an inner ring by sprinkling the scallions inside the ring of tomatoes. Serve immediately.

4. Place the chips in a large basket and watch this appetizer disappear before your eyes.

Note: For a less filling appetizer, omit the layers of beans and cheese.

Serves 8

For a quick dinner, heat the bean and cheese layer in the microwave, then add remaining layers. Serve with either chips or warm rolls.

Barbecued Chicken

My friend Larrie gave me this sauce recipe as a wonderful alternative to tomatoey barbecue sauces, which don't appeal to me. It has been my favorite ever since.

---

2 broiling chickens, cut into quarters, or 8 chicken breast halves

BARBECUE SAUCE
¾ cup cider vinegar
½ cup pineapple or orange juice
½ teaspoon Tabasco
¼ cup Dijon mustard
¼ cup packed brown sugar
¼ cup Worcestershire sauce

⊠⊠⊠⊠⊠⊠⊠⊠⊠⊠

To avoid burning chicken on an open grill, precook the chicken and merely brown it on the grill. However, the slow cooking in a covered grill makes it wonderfully moist.

1. Wash the chicken pieces in cold water and pat dry. Place in a large, shallow glass baking dish; refrigerate.

2. To make the barbecue sauce, place all the ingredients in a small bowl and whisk together until well blended.

3. Pour the sauce over the chicken and turn each piece so it is coated with barbecue sauce. Cover the dish with plastic wrap and refrigerate for about one hour. Remove the chicken from the refrigerator 30 minutes before cooking, turn the pieces again, and let them sit at room temperature.

4. Meanwhile, preheat a gas grill or build a charcoal fire. Turn the gas grill to low or spread out the coals to provide a low, even heat. Remove the chicken from the dish and place the pieces on the grill. With a pastry brush, brush each piece with the barbecue sauce. Turn each piece and brush again. Reserve the remaining sauce. Close the lid of the grill and cook the chicken for 50 to 60 minutes, or until crusty and tender. Brush with the sauce every 15 minutes. If you are cooking the chicken on charcoal, you must watch it carefully and turn it often, so it doesn't burn. The gas grill is highly recommended, because the heat is controlled and the chicken remains tender and moist.

5. Remove the chicken from the grill; place on a serving dish.

6. Either serve hot or let the chicken cool for a few minutes, arrange on a serving platter, and refrigerate until cold. When cold, cover lightly with plastic wrap until ready to serve.

Serves 8

Mixed Bean Salad

This salad uses a mix of beans similar to the Multibean Soup on page 157. You can buy the dried beans in quantity and make up packages of them for soup and salad. They make great hostess gifts, too. A timesaving alternative is to use canned beans.

---

2 cups mixed dried beans (¼ cup each of garbanzo, navy, red kidney, lima, pinto, black turtle, black-eyed peas, and split peas)

4 quarts water

½ pound fresh green beans, trimmed and cut into 1-inch pieces

½ pound fresh wax beans, trimmed and cut into 1-inch pieces

8 scallions, coarsely chopped, with green tops

½ cup finely chopped fresh parsley

VINAIGRETTE

¼ cup white wine vinegar

1 tablespoon sugar

3 large cloves of garlic, minced

1 teaspoon dry mustard

¼ teaspoon salt

freshly ground black pepper

½ cup corn oil

¼ cup olive oil

1. Place the dried beans in a large saucepan and cover with water. Soak overnight or for several hours. Drain and rinse the beans with cold water. Put them back into the saucepan and add 2 quarts of the water. Bring to a rapid boil over high heat. Reduce the heat, cover the pot, and simmer for 1 hour, or until tender. Remove from the heat, drain, rinse, and chill them in a large bowl. If you use canned beans, drain and rinse them. You should have 4 cups of drained beans.

2. Place the remaining 2 quarts of water in a large saucepan and, over high heat, bring to a rapid boil. Add the green beans and wax beans. When the water begins to boil again, cook the beans for 2 minutes, or until tender crisp. Drain the beans and plunge them quickly into ice water to stop the cooking. Drain again and add them to the cooked dried beans.

3. Add the scallions and parsley and gently mix.

4. To MAKE THE VINAIGRETTE, put the vinegar, sugar, garlic, mustard, salt, and several gratings of pepper, to taste into a food processor. Process for 30 seconds. With the motor running, slowly drizzle the oils into the mixture and continue blending until it is thick and creamy.

5. Pour the vinaigrette over the beans, place in a serving bowl, cover with plastic wrap, and chill.

Serves 8

Gramma Bea's Strawberry Shortcake

*Every summer, my mom made this strawberry shortcake for one of
our many neighborhood picnics. To me, it is the essence of June and memory.
The luscious strawberries were freshly picked from our neighbor's
huge garden; the fluffy biscuits still warm from Mom's oven.*

SHORTCAKE

- 2 cups all-purpose flour
- 2 tablespoons sugar
- 4 teaspoons baking powder
- ¼ teaspoon salt
- 4 tablespoons very cold butter
- 1 egg, well beaten
- ⅓ cup light cream

STRAWBERRY FILLING

- 3 quarts fresh, unhulled, unwashed strawberries
- 4 tablespoons sugar

WHIPPED CREAM

- 2 cups heavy cream
- 2 tablespoons Grand Marnier liqueur, or 2 teaspoons vanilla extract

1. Preheat oven to 450°F.

2. TO MAKE THE SHORTCAKE, place the dry ingredients in a food processor. With the steel blade, process briefly. Add the butter to the flour mixture and process until it resembles coarse crumbs.

3. Mix the egg and cream in a small bowl and pour into the flour mixture with the motor running. Process quickly until just blended. Form dough into a ball with your hands.

4. Place the dough on a lightly floured surface and knead about 10 times. Pat or roll the dough to a ½-inch thickness.

5. With a 2½-inch round cookie cutter, cut the dough into rounds and place them on an ungreased baking sheet.

6. Bake the shortcakes for 10 to 12 minutes, or until golden brown. Remove from the baking sheet and cool on a wire rack. When cool, slice the shortcakes in half horizontally, but keep each one intact. Stack them in two layers and wrap them together in aluminum foil. Pack the shortcakes on the top of the picnic basket. The shortcakes can be made well in advance of the picnic and stored in the freezer until the day of the picnic. Just be sure they are thawed before serving. For the best flavor, assemble the dessert while the short-cakes are still warm.

7. TO MAKE THE STRAWBERRY FILLING, on the day of the picnic, place the strawberries in a colander and quickly wash them in cold water. Reserve eight of the best-looking berries and remove the hulls from the rest. Cut the large berries in half or in quarters, so all the pieces are approximately the same size. Place the hulled berries in a 2-quart container with a lid and sprinkle the sugar over them to draw out the juices. Cover the berries and store in the refrigerator until you pack the basket. Place the eight select berries in a resealable plastic bag.

8. TO MAKE THE WHIPPED CREAM, just before leaving for the picnic, place the cream in the medium-sized bowl of an electric mixer and whip at high speed until soft peaks form. Stir in the Grand Marnier. Mound the whipped cream in a container with a tight-fitting lid and pack in a cooler.

Serves 8

• *As the poet William Blake said, "Doubtless God could have made a better berry, but doubtless God never did." For the very best strawberry experience, buy ripe, local berries in season and eat them furiously while they last.*

• *Examine the berries when you get home, discarding any bruised or damaged ones. Blot them and return them to the carton or spread them out in a single layer and cover loosely with paper towels. Use them within two days and enjoy every bite.*

ASSEMBLY

When it is time to present this creation, place a shortcake bottom in each bowl and cover with a generous amount of berries. Place a large spoonful of whipped cream on top of the berries and cover with the shortcake top. Divide the remaining berries among the eight servings, add a little more whipped cream, place a select strawberry on top of each, and serve.

Summer Canoe Picnic

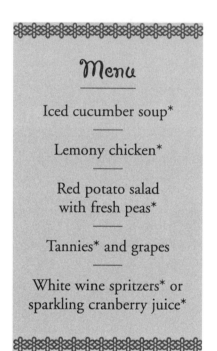

A hot summer day is essential for this adventure. For a mixed age group, pick a lazy stream or river and gently paddle with the current. Wear your bathing suits and take along your sense of humor for the dunking someone in the group is sure to have. Arrange to be picked up at a point downstream, so you don't have to fight the current on the return trip.

The first challenge of a canoeing picnic is to keep the food dry as well as cold. To do this, find a large waterproof bag with a secure closure. Canoe rental outfits will often supply these bags. If you are taking your own canoe, you have probably used your ingenuity to devise waterproof storage. Once you have your gear stowed and are enjoying the gentle flow of the river, you are ready for your second challenge — to find the perfect picnic spot and to have everyone agree to stop *before* you have paddled past it.

What Else to Take

- Waterproof food storage bag
- Corkscrew
- Sunscreen
- Towels
- Lightweight ground cloths

Iced Cucumber Soup

You'll know what "cool as a cucumber" means when you serve this refreshing soup on the hottest day of summer. It is simple to make and divine to eat.

---

5 cucumbers, peeled, seeded, and cut into 1-inch chunks

13 fresh mint leaves

2 cups buttermilk

2 cups chicken stock

1 tablespoon lime juice

½ teaspoon salt

1. Place the cucumbers and 5 of the mint leaves in a blender or food processor and whirl to a fine purée. Pour the purée into a 2-quart pitcher. Add the buttermilk, chicken stock, lime juice, and salt and mix well.

2. Chill the soup for at least 1 hour, until it is icy cold, then pour into thermos bottles. Put the 8 remaining mint leaves in a small plastic bag and garnish each serving with a mint leaf at the picnic.

Serves 8

Which Cucumber?

*F*or best results in this recipe, use dark green slicing cucumbers or the longer greenhouse, or English, variety that has fewer seeds.

Kirby cucumbers are the short, squat pickling variety that are made into dill pickles but sold fresh. Their thin skins and crispness are assets in making slaws and fresh relishes.

Lemony Chicken

Lemon and chicken are a combination made in heaven.

---

12 to 16 chicken thighs, with skin removed

1 cup plus 2 tablespoons lemon juice

1 cup all-purpose flour

½ teaspoon salt

½ teaspoon dried thyme

freshly ground black pepper

2 tablespoons butter

2 tablespoons corn oil

½ cup chicken stock

1 tablespoon grated lemon zest

1. Rinse the chicken in cold water and pat dry. Place in a shallow noncorrosive baking pan and cover with 1 cup of the lemon juice. Marinate in the refrigerator for about two hours, turning several times. Let the chicken sit at room temperature for 30 minutes before cooking.

2. Mix the flour, salt, ¼ teaspoon of the thyme, and pepper to taste in a medium-sized paper bag and shake a few pieces of chicken at a time in the bag until they are evenly coated with the flour mixture.

3. Meanwhile, heat the butter and oil until hot, but not smoking, over medium heat in a large skillet. Arrange chicken thighs in the skillet without crowding, and sauté for about 5 to 10 minutes on each side, or until the pieces are golden brown. Gently remove the chicken from the skillet and place in a large shallow baking pan.

4. Preheat oven to 350°F.

5. Mix the stock with the remaining 2 tablespoons of lemon juice and pour it around the chicken in the baking pan. Sprinkle each piece with a little of the lemon zest and remaining ¼ teaspoon thyme. Bake for 35 to 40 minutes, or until the chicken is cooked through, but not dry. Let sit for about 15 minutes, then store uncovered in the refrigerator. When cold, arrange the chicken on two lightweight picnic serving plates and cover them tightly with plastic wrap. Refrigerate until ready to leave. Pack the plates in an insulated bag with a frozen ice pack.

Serves 8

Red Potato Salad
with Fresh Peas

My husband, Jack, feels that summer isn't complete without at least one batch of this wonderful salad. The sprightly peas provide a nice color and texture to the creamy salad.

---

2 pounds small red potatoes, washed and cut into halves or quarters (about 8 cups — leave the skins on)

1 medium Vidalia or sweet onion, chopped

¼ cup cider vinegar

½ teaspoon salt

¼ cup plain yogurt

2 tablespoons mayonnaise

1 tablespoon Dijon mustard

freshly ground black pepper

4 leaves fresh mint, chopped, or 1 tablespoon minced fresh dill

1 pound fresh peas, shelled

1. Bring a large pot of salted water to a boil. Add the potatoes and cook for 15 minutes or until they are tender when pierced with a sharp knife. Drain the potatoes and place them in a large bowl with the onions, 2 tablespoons of the vinegar, and the salt. Gently stir the potatoes to combine all the ingredients. Cover the bowl with plastic wrap and let it sit unrefrigerated for 30 minutes to blend the flavors.

2. In a small bowl, whisk together the remaining vinegar, the yogurt, mayonnaise, mustard, and pepper to taste just until smooth. Pour this dressing over the marinated potatoes and stir to blend. Sprinkle the mint over the salad and scatter the peas over all. Store the salad in two covered 1-quart containers and chill until ready to pack in an insulated bag for the picnic.

Serves 8

If you miss the season of fresh peas, substitute frozen baby peas.

Tannies

My high school friend Judy's mom always had a cookie jar filled with these luscious graham cracker brownies. I loved them then and still do. And they have been popular with the teens in my life ever since.

---

24 squares graham crackers, rolled into crumbs

½ cup wheat germ

one 14-ounce can sweetened condensed milk

one 6-ounce package chocolate chips

1 teaspoon vanilla extract

½ cup chopped walnuts (optional)

1. Preheat oven to 350°F. Lightly grease a 9-inch square baking pan.

2. Combine the graham cracker crumbs, wheat germ, milk, chocolate chips, vanilla, and walnuts in a large bowl and mix well.

3. Spread the batter in the prepared pan and bake for 35 minutes, or until lightly browned on top. Cool the tannies in the pan for 5 minutes only, then cut into squares and remove from the pan. Cool completely on wire racks. Pack the tannies in a resealable plastic container or bag and place on the top of the pack when it is time to travel.

Serves 8

I can't imagine any leftovers here, but I suggest that you make two batches and freeze one. They will emerge from the freezer in great shape.

White Wine Spritzers

What says summer more clearly than a wine spritzer on a hot day?

---

one 1.5-liter bottle light
    summer wine, chilled
one *1-liter bottle sparkling*
    water, chilled
1 *lemon, thinly sliced*

1. Fill each glass almost half full of wine, top off with sparkling water, and add a slice of lemon.

Serves 8 generously

Light Summer Wines
Try Pinot Grigio, Fumé Blanc, Sauvignon Blanc, or Riesling in your White Wine Spritzers.

Sparkling Cranberry Juice

I always like to include an equally attractive nonalcoholic alternative on picnics, since not everyone likes or can drink alcoholic beverages.

---

one 48-ounce bottle cranberry
    juice cocktail, chilled
one *1-liter bottle sparkling*
    water, chilled
1 *lemon, thinly sliced*

1. Fill each glass almost half full of cranberry juice, top off with sparkling water, and add a slice of lemon.

Serves 8

Berry-Picking Picnic

Menu

Cold berry soup*

———

Fresh country bread and
German black bread

———

Assorted cheese and salami

———

Blueberry-peach tart*

———

Chilled fruit juices,
sparkling water,
or chardonnay

*Recipe included in this chapter

There are those who enjoy picking a berry or two on a nice day and there are those who become compulsive about it. Being of the latter sort, I feel obliged to find ways to make the outing enjoyable for others. This isn't difficult when we pick a sunny Sunday at the height of summer and pack a picnic, beach chairs, and the Sunday paper.

Most berry patches that I know require at least a short hike. This picnic offers a variety of activities and appeals to all ages and dispositions, provided the hike is not too strenuous for the very young or the nonathletic. When you arrive at the chosen spot with a bit of shade and lots of sun, the pickers head for the berry patch and the others stretch out leisurely to read the paper or snooze.

Wine Suggestions

Try an ultrafine California Chardonnay from Edna Valley or Alderbrook or a Rosemount Vineyards Australian Sémillon-Chardonnay.

What Else to Take

For the Food

- Containers for berries
- Water and a strainer for washing berries
- Knives and cutting boards for cheese and salami

Extras

- Bouquet of wildflowers
- Insulated bag
- Beach chairs

Cold Berry Soup

One of the simplest and most refreshing soups of summer, this tangy, creamy mix is very low in calories and is packed with healthful ingredients. It is coolness itself. Use the berries you picked for unbeatable freshness.

3 cups buttermilk
3 cups orange juice
1 tablespoon honey
1 tablespoon lemon juice
dash ground cinnamon
dash ground nutmeg
1 cup washed fresh berries
(blueberries, strawberries,
raspberries, blackberries,
or any combination)

1. Whisk together the buttermilk, orange juice, honey, lemon juice, cinnamon, and nutmeg in a large bowl and chill the soup thoroughly.

2. Pour into a large thermos bottle and put into your pack. Place the berries in a resealable plastic bag and put into the pack. Serve the soup in cups and divide the berries among the cups.

Serves 8

Don't count on a clean, babbling brook near the berry patch. Even if there is one, I advise against drinking the water. Bring along a strainer and plenty of water for washing the berries. They may be just fine, but they also might be dusty from rainstorms.

Blueberry-Peach Tart

*A lavish nutty crust surrounds layers of juicy peaches
and blueberries for this perfect summer treat.*

CRUST

- 1 cup all-purpose flour
- 2 tablespoons sugar
- 5 tablespoons butter or margarine, cut into 1-inch chunks
- 1 egg, beaten
- ½ teaspoon almond extract
- ½ cup finely chopped pecans

PEACH LAYER

- 3 cups peeled and sliced fresh peaches
- 2 tablespoons sugar
- 1 tablespoon lemon juice
- 1 teaspoon cornstarch
- 1 tablespoon butter

BLUEBERRY LAYER

- 4 cups blueberries
- ¼ cup sugar
- 1 tablespoon cornstarch
- 1 teaspoon lemon juice
- dash ground cinnamon
- 1 tablespoon butter

1. TO MAKE THE CRUST, place the flour and sugar in a food processor. Process briefly to mix. Drop the chunks of butter or margarine into the feed tube with the motor running and process quickly until the mixture is crumbly. Add the egg, almond, and pecans and process until just combined. Do not overmix the crust.

2. Form the dough into a flattened ball and press it into the bottom and sides of a 9-inch tart pan with a removable bottom. Chill the crust for 30 minutes.

3. Preheat oven to 350°F.

4. Bake the crust for 15 to 20 minutes, or until slightly brown around the edge. Cool the crust on a wire rack.

5. TO MAKE THE PEACH LAYER, mash the peaches together with the sugar, lemon juice, and cornstarch in a medium saucepan and cook over medium heat for 5 minutes, or until the mixture thickens. Add the butter and stir until blended. Cool slightly and pour into the cooled crust.

6. TO MAKE THE BLUEBERRY LAYER, mash 2 cups of the blueberries with the sugar, cornstarch, lemon juice, and cinnamon and cook in a large saucepan over medium heat for about 10 minutes, or until thickened and translucent. Stir in the butter and the remaining whole blueberries. Cover the peach layer with this blueberry mixture. Leave the tart in the pan and cover tightly with plastic wrap before putting into the pack.

Makes one 9-inch tart

Neighborhood Poolside Picnic

Menu

Hummus* with whole-wheat
or plain pita bread

———

Grilled salmon fillets
with mustard dill sauce*

———

Beet and walnut salad*

———

Vonnie's frosty fruit salad*

———

Butter lettuce
with lemon vinaigrette

———

Crusty French bread
with garlic butter

———

Chocolate zucchini cake*
or chocolate lush*

———

Chilled white zinfandel

*Recipe included in this chapter

When I was growing up, the neighbors shared the work and pleasure of digging and building a swimming pool from scratch. The result was that every summer weekend we shared meals by the pool. Usually, a large piece of meat was communally purchased (before the days of watching our cholesterol) and grilled. Each family contributed salads, desserts, and appetizers that were shared. This is a modern version of our poolside picnics.

Wine Suggestions

Try Glen Ellen or Sutter Home white Zinfandel on the slightly sweet side or Beringer, Deloach, or Beuhler white Zinfandel for those whose taste runs to dry.

What Else to Take

- Charcoal and portable grill, unless you *know* there will be a grill
- Many beach towels
- Pool toys and rafts
- Inflated balls
- Baskets of flowers

Hummus

In the New Jersey suburb where I lived in the 1950s, we had never heard of this classic Mediterranean dish. We are lucky enough now to live in a time when we can enjoy foods from around the world in our own homes.

2	cups lightly drained cooked garbanzo beans
¾	cup tahini†
¼	cup fresh lemon juice
3 to 4	cloves of garlic, minced
½	teaspoon tamari
	freshly ground pepper (optional)
1	package whole-wheat pita bread
1	package plain pita bread

†A smooth paste of sesame seeds.

1. Place the beans, tahini, lemon juice, garlic, and tamari in a blender or food processor and process until smooth and creamy. Add pepper to taste.

2. Place the hummus in a 1-quart covered container. Store in the refrigerator until it's time to pack it in the picnic basket. Hummus also freezes beautifully.

3. Cut the pita bread into 1-inch wedges and place in a plastic bag until packing time. Take a basket for serving the pita bread.

Makes 3 cups

To save time, use a can of garbanzo beans, or chickpeas, instead of cooking them yourself. Garnish with a fresh parsley sprig and a drizzle of olive oil.

Grilled Salmon Fillets
with Mustard Dill Sauce

*Salmon is almost as versatile as chicken, but this smooth,
tangy sauce remains one of my favorites.*

---

4 pounds salmon fillets
   olive oil

SAUCE
½ cup plain yogurt
¼ cup Dijon mustard
2 tablespoons
   mayonnaise
1 tablespoon minced
   fresh dill plus dill
   sprigs for garnish
1 tablespoon lemon juice

1. Rinse the salmon in cold water and dry with paper towels. Place the salmon in a shallow baking pan skin side down

2. TO MAKE THE SAUCE, combine all of the ingredients in a small bowl. Whisk until well blended. Refrigerate until ready to serve.

3. Brush the salmon lightly with the oil and let it reach room temperature.

4. Preheat gas grill at high heat and then turn down to low, or build a medium charcoal fire. Grill the salmon for 7 to 10 minutes on each side, or until the flesh is flaky.

5. Arrange the salmon on a serving plate and garnish with dill sprigs. Serve the sauce on the side. If you prepare the salmon at home, cover the plate with plastic wrap when the fish is cool. Store in the refrigerator. Serve the salmon cold.

Serves 8

• *Atlantic and Pacific farm-raised salmon are excellent, but if you get a chance to eat wild Alaskan salmon, grab it! You'll learn what salmon really tastes like.*

• *Many public beaches do not allow open fires. If you know this is the case or don't know the regulations of the beach you are visiting, prepare the salmon at home and bring it to the picnic.*

Beet and Walnut Salad

Use small tender beets in this simple recipe.
Serve the salad on a nest of shredded beet greens.

1½ pounds small beets,
    trimmed
⅓ cup chopped walnuts
2 tablespoons sherry vinegar
1 tablespoon balsamic
    vinegar
⅓ cup olive oil
2 tablespoons minced parsley
freshly ground black pepper

1. Cook the beets in boiling salted water for about 45 minutes, or until easily pierced with a fork. Drain and let cool.

2. While the beets are cooking, toast the walnuts for 5 to 10 minutes in a toaster oven set at 400°F.

3. When the beets are cool enough to handle, cut off the root and stem ends and slip off the skins. Quarter them and put them into a medium bowl.

4. Combine the vinegars in a small bowl and whisk in the olive oil. Pour the vinaigrette over the warm beets and stir to coat. Sprinkle with nuts and parsley and a few grinds of pepper to taste. Serve in a pretty bowl either warm or at room temperature. Cover the bowl tightly with plastic wrap for trouble-free transport.

Serves 8

Vonnie's Frosty Fruit Salad

The thought of this sweet salad, which Vonnie made several times each summer, recalls hot summer weekends in the 1950s amidst friends and family of all ages. I couldn't resist adding it to this menu.

---

1 tablespoon gelatin

¼ cup cold water

2 teaspoons egg-white powder

¼ cup warm water

½ cup sugar

1 cup heavy cream, whipped

1½ cups red or green seedless grapes

1 cup drained, canned pineapple chunks

½ cup broken walnuts

½ cup plain yogurt

curly endive or escarole for garnish

1. Dissolve the gelatin in the cold water and the egg-white powder in the warm water. Beat the egg-white mixture with a whisk until stiff. Heat gelatin mixture to a boil in a microwave oven, and then slowly pour it over the beaten egg white while whisking. Gradually add the sugar and continue beating for 5 minutes, or until very thick. Cool the mixture in the refrigerator for 15 to 20 minutes.

2. Remove the mixture from the refrigerator and fold in the whipped cream, grapes, pineapple, walnuts, and yogurt. Pour the salad into a 2-quart mold and chill for 2 to 3 hours.

3. Unmold the salad onto a plate just before taking it to the picnic. Decorate the edges with the endive.

Serves 8

A quick alternative to this fruity delight is the classic mix of sour cream and brown sugar served over grapes.

Chocolate Zucchini Cake

*Aren't we always looking for unusual ways to use our abundant zucchini?
Janet Ballantyne came up with this delectable moist chocolate cake for
Garden Way's Joy of Gardening Cookbook (1984).*

CAKE

   4   ounces unsweetened chocolate, melted
   ½   cup vegetable oil
   2   cups sugar
   ½   cup (1 stick) butter, softened
   3   eggs, beaten
   1   tablespoon vanilla extract
   2   cups sifted unbleached all-purpose flour
   ⅓   cup cocoa
   2   teaspoons baking powder
   2   teaspoons baking soda
   1   teaspoon salt
   ⅓   cup buttermilk
   3   cups coarsely grated zucchini
   ½   cup chopped nuts

ICING

   8   ounces softened cream cheese
   6   tablespoons softened butter
   1   pound confectioners' sugar
   2   tablespoons grated orange zest
   1   tablespoon orange juice

1. Preheat oven to 350°F. Grease a 9- by 13-inch pan.

2. TO MAKE THE CAKE, combine the chocolate and oil in a small bowl.

3. In a large bowl, cream the sugar and butter until light and fluffy. Add the eggs and vanilla and beat well. Stir in the chocolate mixture until well blended.

4. Sift the flour, cocoa, baking powder, baking soda, and salt into the batter and add the buttermilk. Stir until the batter is smooth. Mix the zucchini and nuts into the batter.

5. Pour the batter into the prepared pan and bake for 40 minutes, or until a tester inserted into the center of the cake comes out clean. Cool the cake completely on a wire rack.

6. TO MAKE THE ICING, cream the cheese and butter in a medium-sized bowl. Gradually blend in the sugar until well combined. Add the orange zest and juice and mix until smooth.

7. Ice the cooled cake, cut into serving pieces, and place in a rectangular covered plastic container that is deep enough to allow for the icing.

Serves 8

Remember to sift flour before measuring, as the volume changes with sifting.

Chocolate Lush

My mom concocted this family favorite on the tradition of the old-fashioned upside-down cake. It has the added benefit of being a low-cholesterol, low-fat chocolate dessert, despite its rich taste.

1 cup unbleached all-purpose flour

½ cup granulated sugar

¼ cup cocoa

2 teaspoons baking powder

½ teaspoon baking soda

¼ teaspoon salt

½ cup milk

2 tablespoons vegetable oil

1 teaspoon vanilla extract

½ cup chopped walnuts (optional)

TOPPING

1½ cups hot water

½ cup firmly packed light brown sugar

6 tablespoons cocoa

2 tablespoons butter

¼ teaspoon salt

1. Preheat oven to 350°F and grease a 9-inch square baking pan.

2. In a large bowl, sift together the flour, granulated sugar, cocoa, baking powder, baking soda, and salt. Combine the milk, oil, and vanilla in a small bowl, stir into the flour mixture, and mix well. Add the walnuts. Spread the batter in the prepared pan.

3. TO MAKE THE TOPPING, whisk the ingredients together in a small bowl and pour evenly over the batter. The topping will be very soupy. Bake for 45 minutes, or until the cake comes away from the sides of the pan. Cool in the pan on a wire rack. Cut into squares, cover with foil, and bring to the picnic.

Serves 8

Summer in the Berkshires Picnic

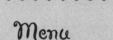

Menu

Shredded carrots
with walnut vinaigrette*

———

Kate's teriyaki
chicken wings*

———

Tortellini salad
with pine nuts*

———

Sour cream chocolate cake*

———

Iced coffee or tea or
chilled white wine

*Recipe included in this chapter

The bucolic Berkshire Hills abound with sheltered glades, flowering meadows, and summer performing arts festivals. Picnicking ranges from the most casual to the well orchestrated. Find a lovely, rural spot near you and use these recipes or buy food from a fabulous food store and have a great day.

Wine Suggestions

Try a Vernaccia di San Gimignano or, on the lighter side, a dry galestro from Antinori or Ricasoli.

What Else to Take

- Blankets
- Beach chairs
- Candles for evening
- Bouquet of wildflowers
- Ground cloth
- Wildflower guide book
- Board game

Shredded Carrots
with Walnut Vinaigrette

Bobbi Crosby, who used to cater in the Berkshires, supplied this yummy, easy recipe.

_____

4 medium carrots, peeled and shredded

¼ cup finely chopped fresh parsley

WALNUT VINAIGRETTE

2 tablespoons white wine vinegar

1 tablespoon Dijon mustard

¼ teaspoon salt

¼ teaspoon sugar

1 clove of garlic, finely minced

2 tablespoons walnut oil

¼ cup peanut oil

1. Place the carrots and parsley in a medium-sized bowl.

2. TO MAKE THE VINAIGRETTE, combine the vinegar, mustard, salt, sugar, and garlic in a small bowl. Slowly whisk in the oils until the dressing is well blended. Pour the vinaigrette over the carrots and stir to combine. Place in a covered serving bowl and chill until ready to take to the picnic.

Serves 8

❌❌❌❌❌❌❌❌❌❌❌❌❌❌❌❌❌❌❌❌❌❌

Raw is easy, but cooking carrots actually increases the sweetness and releases the nutrients. To cook carrots for this recipe, quickly sauté the grated carrots in a teaspoon of butter for a minute or two, or until just wilted.

Kate's Teriyaki Chicken Wings

*This truly tasty dish that my daughter Kate created is simple
to prepare. The secret is a long period of marinating.*

---

16 chicken wings
¼ cup sesame seeds

MARINADE
½ cup sake, mirin (sweet
    cooking sake),† or dry
    white wine
½ cup soy sauce
2 tablespoons brown sugar
1½-inch piece of fresh ginger
    root, peeled and chopped
1 clove garlic, crushed

† Available in natural foods stores

1. Rinse the chicken wings in cold water and pat dry.
Place them in a shallow glass dish.

2. To MAKE THE MARINADE, combine the ingredients in a
medium-sized bowl and pour over the chicken.

3. Let the chicken marinate overnight.

4. Preheat oven to 350°F.

5. Place the chicken in a roasting pan and brush with the
marinade. Sprinkle the wings with the sesame seeds and
bake for 30 minutes, or until they are browned and cooked
through. Let sit for 15 minutes and then place the chicken
on a serving plate and cool in the refrigerator. When cold,
cover the chicken with plastic wrap and transport to the
picnic.

Serves 8

Tortellini Salad
with Pine Nuts

This fragrant combination of tastes and textures is another of Bobbi Crosby's creations. I love the crunch of the pine nuts. Use a good-quality tortellini with a filling you enjoy.

2 pounds fresh tortellini pasta

1 cup seeded and chopped green bell peppers

1 cup seeded and chopped red bell peppers

1 cup chopped scallions, with some green tops

½ cup chopped pine nuts

¼ cup chopped fresh basil

¼ cup chopped fresh dill

¼ cup grated Parmesan cheese

DRESSING

¼ cup balsamic vinegar

1 clove of garlic, minced

¼ teaspoon salt

freshly ground black pepper

¾ cup peanut oil

1. Cook the tortellini according to package directions.

2. Drain the tortellini and place in a large bowl with the peppers, scallions, pine nuts, basil, dill, and Parmesan.

3. TO MAKE THE DRESSING, combine the vinegar, garlic, salt, and pepper to taste in a small bowl. Whisk in the oil until well combined. Pour the dressing over the tortellini and chill. Put the salad into a 2-quart covered bowl to take to your picnic.

Serves 8 generously

Known to Italians as pignoli, these mild, crunchy seeds from pinecones are an important ingredient in Mediterranean cuisine, from pastas to salads to desserts. They're known in Native American cooking as pine nuts or Indian nuts.

Sour Cream Chocolate Cake

There is nothing low-fat or light about this moist, delicious cake, which is another contribution from Bobbi Crosby's kitchen.

---

  1 cup all-purpose flour
  1 teaspoon baking powder
  ½ teaspoon baking soda
  ½ teaspoon salt
1 ¼ cups sugar
  2 ounces unsweetened
     chocolate
  1 tablespoon cocoa
  ⅓ cup boiling water
  2 eggs
  ¾ cup (1½ sticks) unsalted
     butter, softened
  ½ cup sour cream
  1 teaspoon vanilla extract

ICING
  ½ cup heavy cream
  6 ounces semisweet or
     bittersweet chocolate, cut
     into medium-sized pieces

1. Preheat oven to 325°F. Grease and flour an 8-inch springform pan.

2. In a large bowl, sift together the flour, baking powder, baking soda, and salt. Set aside.

3. Place ¼ cup of the sugar, the chocolate, and the cocoa in a food processor. Process the mixture until it resembles coarse crumbs. Add the water and process until the chocolate melts, then add the eggs and process until combined. Add the butter, sour cream, and vanilla and process again. Finally, add the remaining 1 cup sugar and the flour mixture and process until well blended.

4. Pour the batter into the prepared pan. Bake for 50 to 55 minutes, or until the cake comes away from the sides of the pan.

5. Cool in the pan for about 10 minutes before removing the sides and bottom of the pan. Cool the cake on a wire rack. When completely cool, ice the cake on the rack so the excess icing can run off.

6. TO MAKE THE ICING, scald the cream in a heavy saucepan over medium heat. Add the chocolate and stir the mixture over the heat for 1 minute. Remove the icing from the heat and continue to stir until the chocolate is completely melted. When the icing is warm, not hot, spread it on the cake. Place the iced cake on a plate and store in a cool place, so the icing can set, then place it in a basket for the picnic.

Serves 8

Summer at the Beach Picnic

Menu

Phyllo turnovers*

Grilled tuna with lime*

Garden fresh tomatoes with
basil and balsamic vinegar*

Marinated pasta salad*

Fresh peach ice cream* and
Omi's cocoa cake*

Selection of cold beer

Sparkling water

Mix of lemonade and
iced tea in a big thermal jug

*Recipe included in this chapter

For this classic picnic of the summer, imagine a clear, hot, dry day with an intense blue sky reflected off the water, and white sand. The endless crashing of waves on the beach is the musical background for your day in the sun. Put food, young people of all ages, and a stretch of beach together and you have the ingredients of a perfect picnic. Add sunshine, a shady spot, some dune grass, blankets, and beach toys, and be prepared for a great day. Whether you're on wide, wild stretches of the Pacific Coast, an East Coast beach, or a rocky shore, a sense of peace and relaxation comes from being close to the sea.

What Else to Take

For the Food

- Water bottles
- Cutting board
- Sharp knife
- Picnic platter for tuna
- Hibachi
- Charcoal
- Matches

Extras

- Sunscreen
- Plenty of beach towels
- Beach chairs
- Blankets
- Paddleball and beach toys
- Beach umbrellas
- Some kind of cart to carry all this stuff from the car to the beach

Phyllo Turnovers

While these are somewhat labor intensive, they freeze beautifully if wrapped carefully. I usually freeze some before baking if I know I won't use the whole batch.

---

1 tablespoon olive oil

1 medium onion, chopped

3 cups finely chopped broccoli or cauliflower

1 cup grated Cheddar cheese

1 slice dry Swedish rye bread, crumbled

1 egg

1 tablespoon lemon juice

½ teaspoon salt

¼ teaspoon white pepper

½ 1-pound package phyllo dough

½ cup melted butter

2 tablespoons fennel seeds

1. In a medium-sized skillet, heat the oil and sauté the onion until soft. Place the onion in a large bowl.

2. Steam the broccoli for 5 to 10 minutes, until tender but still bright green. Add the broccoli to the onion. Mix in the Cheddar, bread crumbs, egg, lemon juice, salt, and pepper and set aside the broccoli mixture.

3. Preheat oven to 375°F.

4. Before opening the phyllo dough, clear a work surface that is approximately 2½- by 2-feet. Have a clean, damp dish towel or plastic wrap available for covering the phyllo. Place the butter within reach, as well as a baking sheet. Open the phyllo and lay one sheet on the work surface with the long side facing you. Lightly brush the sheet with melted butter; place another sheet of phyllo on top of the first and brush it with butter. Repeat this process once more, so you have three layers of phyllo. Cover the remaining phyllo with the damp cloth or plastic wrap so it won't dry out.

5. With scissors, cut the layered dough crosswise into six equal strips. One inch from the end of each strip near you, place a heaping tablespoon of the filling. Fold a triangle of the dough over the filling and continue to fold the dough as if you were folding a flag. Place the triangle on a baking sheet, lightly brush with butter, and sprinkle with a few fennel seeds. Repeat this procedure until you have about 30 triangles. Bake for 15 minutes, or until golden brown. Cool the triangles on wire racks and pack them gently in a covered tin to transport to the picnic. These can be made ahead and frozen either before or after baking.

Serves 8

Working with Phyllo

Phyllo dough is available in the freezer section of most supermarkets. It is carefully wrapped to keep air from drying the paper-thin layers of dough. When brushed with melted butter and stacked, wrapped around a delicacy and baked, the result is divine. In addition to this recipe, phyllo is used in the classic Middle Eastern dessert, baklava, and the Greek spinach pie, spanakopita, and for tiny turnovers of spinach or cheese and rice. The possibilities are endlessly delicious.

The secret to working with phyllo is to keep it from drying out and becoming brittle. Either cover it carefully with plastic wrap or, for a longer recipe than this, cover it with a damp, but not wet, tea towel. Leftover sheets of dough can be tightly wrapped and stored in the freezer for up to a month without getting crumbly.

Grilled Tuna
with Lime

*Fresh tuna is a wonderfully firm fish with a fairly
low fat content. It is also a popular fish for sushi.*

2½ to 3 *pounds tuna steaks,*
     ¾ inch thick
1 *cup marinade used for
  Chicken Fillets (see
  page 15)*
2 *limes, cut into wedges*

1. Rinse the tuna and pat dry. Place in a shallow container with a tight-fitting cover. Pour the marinade over the tuna, cover the dish, and pack in the cooler. Place the lime wedges in a plastic bag.

2. When you get to the beach, start a charcoal fire in the hibachi. When the coals are hot, grill the tuna 5 to 7 minutes on each side, or until cooked through. Brush frequently with the marinade. Place the tuna on a picnic platter and surround with the lime wedges.

Serves 8

**If you prefer, or if you can't
cook on the beach, grill the
tuna at home, chill it, and
serve it cold.**

Garden-Fresh Tomatoes
with Basil and Balsamic Vinegar

This simple dish is totally dependent on fresh garden tomatoes and fresh basil and the rich taste of balsamic vinegar. Genetically engineered tomatoes that last in the supermarket for a week cannot be substituted. It is a summer treat for tomato lovers.

---

4 large fresh garden tomatoes
8 leaves fresh basil
½ cup balsamic vinegar

XXXXXXXXXX

Competition for fresh tomatoes comes from the restoration of "heirloom" tomatoes to their rightful place in the market. Many markets feature these interesting-looking tomatoes. I recommend trying Brandywine, a large, rosy pink variety that comes close to Jersey beefsteaks, or the cute little green striped-zebra tomatoes.

1. Wash the tomatoes, remove the tops, and place the tomatoes in a shallow covered dish with the basil leaves. Measure out the vinegar and place it in a small jar with a tight-fitting lid. Pack a small cutting board and your tomato-cutting knife.

2. At the picnic, just before serving, slice the tomatoes into ¼- to ½-inch slices and arrange in the shallow dish. Chop the basil. Drizzle the vinegar over the tomatoes and sprinkle with the basil. So simple and so good.

Note: Casks of balsamic vinegar are family heirlooms in Modena, Italy. This vinegar is available to us in specialty food stores and is extremely expensive. But don't despair! Many nontraditional vinegars are quite tasty and are readily available.

Serves 8

Marinated Pasta Salad

This old standby is a winner at any picnic. It has taste, tang, and travelability.

¾ *pound tricolor rotelle pasta*

⅓ *cup olive oil*

⅓ *cup red wine vinegar*

½ *teaspoon salt*

1 *medium green bell pepper, seeded and chopped*

¼ *cup seeded and chopped red bell pepper*

1 *small purple onion, chopped*

½ *cup minced fresh parsley*

¼ *cup marinated artichoke hearts*

¼ *cup sliced black olives*

4 to 5 *leaves fresh basil, chopped*

freshly ground black pepper

1. In a large pot of boiling salted water, over high heat, cook the pasta for 15 minutes, or until al dente. Drain the pasta in a colander and rinse quickly with cold water.

2. Place the pasta in a large bowl and toss with the oil, vinegar, and salt. Chill the pasta for 1 hour.

3. Meanwhile, prepare the peppers, onion, parsley, artichoke hearts, olives, and basil. When the pasta is cold, add those ingredients and toss well. Grind pepper to taste over all and mix again. Store the salad in a 2-quart covered container in the refrigerator until packing time.

Serves 8

Pick a Pasta

Pasta comes in an almost infinite variety of sizes and shapes. Each one lends itself to a particular type of dressing or sauce. For pasta salads, spiral shaped pastas hold a vinagrette very well. Tubular pastas such as macaroni, penne, or ziti attach themselves nicely to creamy dressings.

Fresh Peach Ice Cream

*M*odern technology allows us to take fresh homemade ice cream to the beach with ease. The secret is having the type of ice-cream maker with a metal container filled with a supercoolant. You place the container in the freezer overnight and it becomes so cold that the ice-cream mixture freezes on contact. The metal container fits into a large cup with a churn. This entire apparatus can be stored in the freezer until packing time and then placed in the cooler for transporting to the beach.

---

2 cups half-and-half

1 cup milk

3 fresh peaches, peeled, chopped, and mashed

¾ cup sugar

¼ teaspoon vanilla extract

a freezer-cylinder type ice-cream maker

1. Place all of the ingredients in a large bowl and stir until well combined.

2. Pour the mixture into the supercold metal container and follow the manufacturer's directions for churning. Store the ice cream in the freezer until packing time. Wrap the entire ice-cream maker in a tablecloth and put it into the picnic cooler. Ours sat in 90°F heat for three hours one day and the ice cream was still frozen when we ate it.

Serves 8

Omi's Cocoa Cake

My grandmother, whom we called Omi instead of the German Oma, loved good food but did not particularly like to cook. She did manage a few specialties. Here is her easily prepared version of a German torte, which her friends enjoyed at many an afternoon kaffeeklatsch, an informal social gathering for coffee and conversation.

CAKE

- 1 cup sugar
- 2 tablespoons butter, softened
- ½ cup cold water
- 2 tablespoons cocoa
- 2 eggs, well beaten
- 1 teaspoon vanilla extract
- 1 cup all-purpose flour
- 1 teaspoon baking powder

FILLING

- 1 cup milk
- ¾ cup sugar
- ¼ cup cocoa
- 2 tablespoons butter, softened
- 1 cup heavy cream, whipped

1. Preheat oven to 350°F.

2. TO MAKE THE CAKE, cream the sugar and butter in a large bowl until thoroughly blended. With a whisk, beat in the water, cocoa, eggs, and vanilla until the mixture is well mixed.

3. Sift the flour and baking powder together into a small bowl and stir into the cocoa mixture. Pour the batter into two greased and floured 9-inch round cake pans and bake for 15 to 20 minutes, or until a tester inserted into the center comes out clean. Cool the cakes on wire racks in the pans for 10 minutes. Remove from the pans and continue cooling on wire racks.

4. TO MAKE THE FILLING, place the milk, sugar, cocoa, and butter in a large saucepan and cook over medium heat for 10 to 15 minutes, or until the mixture thickens. Stir occasionally in the beginning and constantly at the end. Remove from the heat and continue stirring while the mixture is cooling. The filling will resemble a fudge sauce.

5. Place one of the layers upside down on a plate and cover the top with the filling. Carefully place the second layer on top of the filling. Cover the top layer with the whipped cream. Put the cake into a covered box for transporting to the picnic. Store in the refrigerator until travel time.

Serves 8

Music Festival Picnic

Menu

Cold zucchini soup*

Chinese chicken salad
with fried won tons*

Fresh peaches and
pecan bars*

Sun tea*
or chilled white wine

*Recipe included in this chapter

What Else to Take

- Candles and candlesticks,
  silver preferred
- Hurricane lamps are helpful,
  if there is a breeze
- Linen napkins and tablecloth
- China and glassware
- Bouquet of flowers

$\int$ummer music festivals abound — Tanglewood in the Berkshires, Ravinia north of Chicago, Wolf Trap outside Washington, D.C., — in all parts of the country. Competition can be fierce for elegant picnics on the grassy lawns of these outdoor concert halls. What can be more elegant than dining in style to live symphony music on a star-filled evening? Here is the opportunity to use the silver candlesticks, the linen tablecloth and napkins, and the crystal. Transporting these fragile items requires care in packing and serving while outdoors. Plan to pack the china and crystal in extra napkins. Arrange them in a picnic basket with the most fragile items on top. For an elegant picnic, be extravagant in the show you put on. Always have fresh flowers, and in the evening, candlelight is a must. For the food, looking good is almost as important as tasting good. Take care with the presentation.

Wine Suggestions

Try a Vernaccia di San Gimignano from Italy or a lush California or Australian chardonnay.

Cold Zucchini Soup

This fine-flavored soup that will surely please your palate is also easy to make.

---

3 medium zucchini, cut into 2-inch chunks

1 medium onion, chopped

1 bay leaf

1 sprig of parsley

1 sprig of thyme, or 1 teaspoon dried thyme

4½ cups chicken stock (homemade, if possible)

1½ cups plain yogurt

1 tablespoon lemon juice

½ teaspoon salt

¼ teaspoon white pepper

sprigs of fresh thyme (optional)

1. Place the zucchini, onion, bay leaf, parsley, and thyme in a medium-sized saucepan with 1 cup of the chicken stock and bring to a boil over high heat. Simmer the mixture for about 10 minutes, or until the zucchini is tender. Remove the bay leaf, parsley, and thyme and purée the mixture in a blender or food processor until it is of uniform consistency.

2. For a smooth soup, strain the purée by pressing it through a strainer or sieve with the back of a spoon. An unstrained soup will have a slight texture. Add the remaining chicken stock, yogurt, lemon juice, salt, and pepper and stir well to blend. Pour the soup into a 1½-quart covered container; chill for at least 1 hour before packing in the cooler.

3. Garnish each serving with a sprig of thyme, if desired.

Serves 8

For a lovely summer vegetable, cook the zucchini as directed and flavor with salt and pepper. Serve warm with a sprinkling of Parmesan cheese or cold with lemon juice.

Chinese Chicken Salad
with Fried Won Tons

*Larrie contributed this salad to one of our Tanglewood picnics.
We loved it. Over the years, it has evolved somewhat, but the essence has
remained the same. This salad became the mainstay of my picnic business.
It's fun to take on a picnic, because it has so many parts.*

---

2 tablespoons sesame oil

4 slices fresh ginger root,
  peeled and minced

1 clove of garlic

8 chicken breast halves
  (slightly frozen to ease
  cutting), skinned, boned,
  and cut into ¼- by-2-inch
  strips

4 scallions, cut into 1-inch
  julienne with some green
  tops

¼ cup sesame seeds

¼ cup slivered almonds

¼ head red leaf lettuce,
  washed, dried, and
  shredded

1. Heat the 2 tablespoons of sesame oil over medium heat in a wok. Quickly brown the ginger and garlic. Remove them from the wok and discard. Add the chicken in several batches and stir-fry for 2 minutes per batch, or until the chicken pieces are just cooked through. Remove the cooked chicken from the wok and place in a large bowl.

2. Add the scallions, sesame seeds, and almonds to the chicken and toss to mix well. Place the lettuce in a resealable plastic bag and store in the refrigerator until packing time. Pack it in the top part of the cooler.

RECIPE CONTINUES ON NEXT PAGE

DRESSING

- 2 tablespoons soy sauce
- 2 tablespoons rice vinegar
- 1 tablespoon lemon juice
- 1 tablespoon dry mustard
- 2 teaspoons mirin (sweet cooking sake)†
- 1 teaspoon peeled and grated ginger root
- 1 clove of garlic, minced
- ½ teaspoon salt
  freshly ground black pepper
- ½ cup corn oil
- ¼ cup sesame oil

FRIED WON TONS

- ½ cup sesame oil (not the hot variety)
- ½ package won ton skins, cut into ¼-inch strips

†Available in natural foods stores

3. TO MAKE THE DRESSING, place the soy sauce, vinegar, lemon juice, mustard, mirin, ginger root, garlic, salt, and pepper to taste in a blender or food processor and process until well blended. With the motor running, slowly drizzle in the corn and sesame oils and process until the dressing is creamy. Pour the dressing over the chicken and toss. Place the salad in a large covered bowl and chill in the refrigerator until time to pack in the cooler.

4. TO FRY THE WON TONS, wipe out the wok with a paper towel and heat the ½ cup of sesame oil in the wok over medium-high heat. Test the oil temperature by adding one piece of won ton to it. If it burns immediately, the oil is too hot. If the won ton skin quickly turns a golden brown and puffs up slightly, the temperature is perfect. Add three or four pieces of won ton at a time and brown them. Remove the crispy brown won ton skins from the wok: drain on paper towels. When all the won tons are cooked, place them in a plastic bag; pack them on the top of the picnic basket.

5. When it is time to serve the salad, place a bed of lettuce in the center of each plate and spoon a generous portion of chicken on top of the lettuce. Crumble a handful of the crispy won tons on top of the salad and enjoy a taste and texture treat. The remaining won tons can be munched on throughout the meal.

Serves 8

Pecan Bars

*A bakery in Montclair, New Jersey, where I grew up, made a
divine pecan bar that we always had at family tea parties.
This is my attempt at re-creating them, and it's pretty close.*

¾ cup (1½ sticks) butter,
   softened

½ cup sugar

1 egg

1 teaspoon grated lemon zest

1 teaspoon vanilla extract

2 cups all-purpose flour

¼ teaspoon salt

TOPPING

2¼ cups finely chopped pecans

¾ cup sugar

4 egg whites, lightly beaten,
   at room temperature

1 teaspoon ground cinnamon

1. Preheat oven to 350°F.

2. In a large bowl, cream the butter and sugar until light
and fluffy. Add the egg, lemon zest, and vanilla and mix well.

3. Sift the flour and salt into a medium-sized bowl and
add the mixture to the creamed ingredients in small
amounts. Mix until well combined. Spread the dough
evenly in a 15- by 10- by 1-inch pan and bake for 15 minutes, or until lightly browned around the edges.

4. TO MAKE THE TOPPING, combine all of the ingredients
in a large, heavy saucepan and cook over low heat, stirring
constantly, for 2 minutes, or until the sugar is dissolved.
Increase the heat to medium high and continue to cook and
stir for 2 to 3 minutes, or until the mixture thickens,
browns lightly, and comes away from the sides of the pan.

5. Spread the topping evenly over the top of the dough
and bake for 15 minutes longer. Cool in the pan for 5 minutes, and then cut into ¾- by 2-inch bars.

6. Pack the bars in an airtight tin for carrying to
the picnic.

Serves 8

Sun Tea

What is a sunny summer day without a big jar of sun tea sitting on the back steps?

6 tea bags, or 6 tablespoons
   loose tea

3 quarts cold water

¼ cup sugar or honey
   (optional)

2 sprigs of mint (optional)

1 lemon, thinly sliced
   (optional)

1. Place the tea in a 1-gallon glass jar and add the water. Set the jar in a sunny window or outside in the sunshine for several hours until the tea has infused the water.

2. Strain the tea, add your choice of optional ingredients, and chill. Remove the lemon and mint and pour the tea into chilled thermos bottles and take to your picnic.

Makes 3 quarts

Make ice cubes from tea! They make a great conversation piece and won't dilute the tea's flavor. Place the cubes in a plastic bag, then wrap them in a clean tea towel and many layers of newspaper and take them to the picnic in a cooler or insulated bag.

Champagne Tea Picnic

Menu

Cucumber sandwiches
and tomato sandwiches*

Petite lobster rolls*

Rhubarb conserve*
with miniature muffins*

Tante Lulu's apple cake*

Almond rings*

Fresh strawberries
and cream

Tea, lemon water,
or champagne

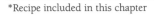

*Recipe included in this chapter

*I*magine setting out an elegant afternoon tea in the fresh air. Tea al fresco may offer you a new experience. Find a lovely spot under a shady tree and take in the tradition of English country homes.

Wine Suggestions

An ultrafine Champagne such as Dom Pérignon or Perrier-Jouët Fleur de Champgane or Taittinger Comtes de Champagne. Prosecco, an Italian sparkling white wine that is lighter than Champagne and not quite as bubbly, is also a wonderful choice.

What Else to Take

- A table and chairs, if you wish to emulate the British
- Linen tablecloth and napkins
- Flowers
- China, silverware, and glassware
- Croquet set

Cucumber Sandwiches and Tomato Sandwiches

How can we possibly have a tea party without finger sandwiches?

---

1 loaf uncut bread

4 tablespoons butter, softened

8 ounces cream cheese, softened

1 cucumber, peeled and thinly sliced

freshly ground black pepper

3 medium tomatoes, cored, peeled, and cut into quarters

salt

1. Thinly slice the bread into 16 slices. Spread each piece of bread out to the edge with a thin layer of butter. Trim the crusts off the slices of bread, so that the edges are straight.

2. Spread eight of the bread slices with a thin layer of cream cheese.

3. On four of these cream cheese slices, arrange the cucumbers, and sprinkle with pepper to taste. Top all four with a buttered slice of bread and, with a sharp knife, cut each sandwich into quarters.

4. Remove everything from the tomato quarters except the outer layer of the tomato. On each of the remaining four cream cheese slices of bread, arrange three of these tomato pieces, which will have no seeds or juice and will be relatively flat. Sprinkle the tomatoes with salt and pepper to taste and cover with a buttered slice. Again, cut each sandwich into quarters.

5. Place all of the sandwiches on a pretty platter, cover with plastic wrap, and store in the refrigerator until teatime. At serving time, garnish the platter with a flower.

Makes 32 finger sandwiches

To save a little time, buy a loaf of thinly sliced bread, cut off the crusts, and make the sandwiches.

Petite Lobster Rolls

The best lobster rolls have the most lobster. Authentic Maine lobster rolls are served on the kind of hot dog rolls with the sides sliced off. For our mini rolls, we will use small finger rolls.

---

4 cups cooked lobster meat
½ cup chopped celery
4 scallions, chopped, with some green tops
1 tablespoon butter, melted
1 tablespoon lemon juice
1 cup mayonnaise
16 small finger rolls

1. Combine the lobster, celery, scallions, butter, and lemon juice in a medium-sized bowl and stir to blend.

2. Gently mix the mayonnaise into the lobster until all pieces are coated.

3. Slice the rolls lengthwise and divide the lobster among the rolls. Arrange them on a pretty plate with the other finger sandwiches.

Serves 8

These are best made by the sea, where you can easily buy cooked lobster meat. Otherwise, have lobster the night before and cook extra for the rolls.

Rhubarb Conserve

This old family favorite is also delicious with hot or cold meats.

---

1 quart rhubarb, cut into
   1-inch pieces

2¼ cups sugar

1 lemon, unpeeled, finely
   chopped

1 orange, unpeeled, finely
   chopped

1 cup raisins

½ cup coarsely chopped
   walnuts

1. Place all of the ingredients in a large stainless steel or nonreactive pot and stir to mix. Let the mixture stand overnight. In the morning, bring the mixture to a boil and cook over medium heat for 15 to 20 minutes, or until thick.

2. Place 2 cups of the conserve in a pretty jar and refrigerate until packing time. Store the remaining conserve in covered containers in the freezer.

Makes 5 cups

When rhubarb is in season, make several batches and give this conserve as hostess or holiday gifts.

Miniature Muffins

These eggless muffins are quite delicious.

1⅔ cups all-purpose flour

¾ cup sugar

⅓ cup wheat germ

½ teaspoon baking soda

¼ teaspoon baking powder

1¼ cups buttermilk

3 tablespoons butter, melted

1. Preheat oven to 400°F. Grease 30 small-sized muffin-pan cups.

2. Into a large bowl, sift together the flour, sugar, wheat germ, baking soda, and baking powder.

3. Combine the buttermilk and butter, add to the flour mixture, and stir until the mixture is just moistened.

4. Pour the batter into the prepared pans and bake for 12 to 15 minutes, or until the muffins are slightly browned on the edges.

5. Cool for a few minutes on a wire rack before removing the muffins from the pans.

Makes 30 small muffins

If you make the standard-sized muffin with this recipe, bake for 20 minutes.

Tante Lulu's Apple Cake

*T ante Lulu, a dear friend of my grandmother's, served this lovely
cake when we visited her in her old brownstone in Hoboken, New Jersey.
The warmth and humor in her eyes as she told her wonderful stories
are as vivid to me as the taste of this cake.*

CRUST

1½ cups all-purpose flour
  1 cup (2 sticks) butter,
     softened
  3 tablespoons sugar
  1 egg yolk, lightly beaten

FILLING

  6 cups apples, peeled, cored,
     and thinly sliced
  ¾ cup sugar
  2 tablespoons lemon juice
  1 tablespoon butter

1. TO MAKE THE CRUST, place the flour, butter, sugar, and
egg yolk in a large bowl and mix with a wooden spoon until
the ingredients are combined.

2. Pat the dough into the bottom and up the sides of a 9-
inch springform pan. Chill the dough for 2 hours.

3. TO MAKE THE FILLING, place all of the ingredients in a
large pot. Stir the mixture to blend and let sit for 5 minutes
to draw the juice from the apples. Cover the pot and steam
the apples over low heat for 5 minutes, or until they are
slightly soft. Cool the apples to room temperature in the pot.

4. Preheat oven to 325°F.

5. Pour the steamed apples into the chilled crust and
bake for 1 hour, or until lightly browned around the edge.
Cool the cake on a wire rack for 10 minutes. Remove the
outer pan ring and cool the cake completely. Leave the cake
on the pan bottom, place on a lace or paper doily, and put
into a covered box for transporting to the picnic.

Serves 8

Almond Rings

An elegant little cookie that is as comfortable on the tea table as in the picnic basket.

¾ cup (1½ sticks) butter, softened

¼ cup sugar

1 egg yolk

½ teaspoon almond extract

2 cups all-purpose flour

¼ teaspoon salt

1 egg white, lightly beaten

½ cup ground almonds

1. In a large bowl, place the butter, sugar, egg yolk, and almond extract and mix well with a wooden spoon. Add the flour and salt. Mix thoroughly until the mixture is well blended.

2. Chill the dough for 1 hour.

3. Preheat oven to 350°F.

4. Break off pieces of the dough the size of a walnut and roll into long rolls like thick pencils. Form the dough into rings and dip in the egg white. Sprinkle the almonds on top and place on an ungreased baking sheet. Bake for 10 minutes, or until lightly browned. Remove from the baking sheet and cool on a wire rack. Pack in a tightly covered container.

Makes 16 rings

Traveling Tea Party

Make a gift of a tea party for a friend. Find a pretty basket, line it with a tea towel, and fill the basket with the muffins, conserve, and cookies from the menu. Add a selection of teas and a small teapot.

Garden Picnic

Menu

Cold carrot soup*

Mediterranean
chicken salad*

Dilly bread*

Food for the gods*

Chilled white wine

*Recipe included in this chapter

𝒶 public garden may not be the ideal spot for your picnic. Instead, select a secluded private garden, possibly in your own backyard or in a field of wildflowers. Let the artist Monet be your inspiration in creating an elegant garden picnic.

Wine Suggestions
Try a fine Soave or Pinot Grigio from northern Italy or a Corvo white from Sicily

What Else to Take

- Small bowls for soup
- Flowers, or a vase if you want to pick them there
- Insect repellent

Cold Carrot Soup

Whether perfumed with ginger or dill, this soup is excellent hot or cold.

---

3   cups peeled and sliced
   carrots

½   cup water

1   medium onion, chopped

1   tablespoon butter

1   tablespoon vegetable oil

3   cups chicken stock
   (homemade, if possible)

1   teaspoon peeled and grated
   fresh ginger root, or 1
   tablespoon finely minced
   fresh dill

¾   teaspoon salt

¼   teaspoon white pepper

1   cup plain yogurt

dill sprigs for garnish

1. Cook the carrots in the water in a microwave oven for 5 minutes, or until tender.

2. Sauté the onion in the butter and oil in a small skillet over medium heat.

3. Pour half of the carrots and onions into a blender with 1 cup of the chicken stock and purée until smooth. Transfer the purée to a large bowl or plastic container with a cover. Pour the remaining carrot mixture, 1 more cup of the chicken stock, the ginger root, salt and pepper into the blender; purée until smooth. Combine the batches and mix well.

4. Stir the remaining chicken stock and yogurt into the soup and chill for 2 hours in a covered plastic container. At the picnic, serve the soup in small bowls and garnish each with a sprig of dill.

Serves 8

Keeping Ginger Root

Store leftover ginger root, carefully wrapped in plastic, in the freezer. When ready to use, grate as much as you need from the frozen root. You will be amazed at the fresh taste. Unfrozen, ginger root keeps in the vegetable drawer of the refrigerator for several weeks.

Mediterranean Chicken Salad

My friend Jean shared this wonderful summer salad, which captures the flavors of the Mediterranean. It has been adapted over the years, but remains one of my summertime favorites.

---

8 chicken breast halves

1 medium green bell pepper, seeded and cut into ½-inch chunks

1 small red bell pepper, seeded and cut into ½-inch chunks

1 medium purple onion, cut into ¼-inch chunks

½ cup pitted black olives

¼ cup artichoke hearts

4 leaves fresh basil, chopped

¼ teaspoon salt

freshly ground black pepper

6 tablespoons balsamic vinegar

6 tablespoons corn oil

6 tablespoons olive oil

1. Place the chicken breasts in a large pot and barely cover with cold water. Bring the water to a boil over high heat. Reduce the heat and simmer the chicken for 20 minutes, or until it is just cooked through. Let the chicken cool slightly in the liquid.

2. When the chicken can be handled, remove the meat from the bones and cut it into 1-inch chunks. Place the chicken in a large bowl.

3. Add the peppers, onion, olives, artichoke hearts, basil, salt, and pepper to taste to the chicken and stir well. Sprinkle the vinegar and oils over all and stir again. Place the salad in a large covered container and chill in the refrigerator until it is time to pack it in the cooler.

Serves 8

Dilly Bread

This award-winning yeast bread that is baked in a bowl is always a big favorite. It is almost a meal in itself. Have it with a salad for a perfect lunch.

¼ cup warm (110°F) water

1 tablespoon active dry yeast

1 cup low-fat cottage cheese

2 tablespoons dill seeds

2 tablespoons sugar

1 tablespoon butter or margarine, softened

1 tablespoon minced dried onion

¼ teaspoon baking soda

1 egg, lightly beaten

2¼ to 2½ cups all-purpose flour

For a great lunch, add a slab of Cheddar cheese to a thick slice of dilly bread and sit under a shady tree with a clinking glass of iced tea.

1. Sprinkle the yeast over the water in a large bowl and let it dissolve.

2. In a medium-sized saucepan, gently heat the cottage cheese over low heat until lukewarm, stirring constantly. Add the dill, sugar, butter, onion, baking soda, and egg to the cottage cheese. Stir well.

3. Add the cheese mixture to the yeast and mix well. Gradually add the flour, ½ cup at a time, beating with a wooden spoon after each addition. Knead the dough about 10 times in the bowl to work the last of the flour into the dough.

4. Shape the dough into a ball and cover the bowl with a damp cloth. Let the dough rise for about 1 hour, or until it is double in size. Grease a 1½-quart round casserole. Punch down the dough and again shape it into a ball. Place it in the prepared casserole and let it rise for 30 to 40 minutes longer.

5. Preheat oven to 350°F.

6. Bake for 40 to 50 minutes, or until lightly browned on top and hollow sounding when tapped. Let the bread rest in the casserole for about 5 minutes before removing it. Cool completely on a wire rack before slicing. Wrap the sliced loaf in a plastic bag and pack in your picnic basket when ready.

Makes 1 loaf

Food for the Gods

*This ambrosial dessert was one from my mother's extensive repertoire
that I loved while growing up. It's easy, delicious, and even
quite healthy if you skip the whipped cream.*

---

3 egg yolks, beaten

7 graham crackers, rolled
into crumbs

1 cup chopped pecans

½ cup chopped pitted dates

½ cup sugar

1 teaspoon baking powder

3 egg whites, beaten until
stiff peaks form

1 cup heavy cream, whipped
(optional)

1. Preheat oven to 350°F and grease a 9- by 13-inch baking pan.

2. Place the egg yolks in a large bowl. Add the graham cracker crumbs, pecans, dates, sugar, and baking powder and mix well. Gently fold the egg whites into the crumb mixture until combined.

3. Pour the batter into the prepared pan. Bake for 15 to 20 minutes, or until lightly browned. Cool on a wire rack for 10 minutes before cutting.

4. Put the pieces on a plate and cover with plastic wrap for traveling to the picnic. Bring the whipped cream in a covered container and add a dollop to each piece before serving.

Serves 8 generously

Sunlight Through the Trees Picnic

Menu

Crostini*

Tortellini chicken salad*

Citrus salad*

Blueberry muffins*

Lemon sand torte with fruit*

Chilled white wine

*Recipe included in this chapter

D eep woods with tall trees filter the sunlight onto soft grass in a sheltered glade. A meandering stream gently gurgling over rocks provides the background music. You are at the perfect secluded spot for a romantic picnic.

Wine Suggestions

Try a fine Muscadet or a dry Chenin Blanc from Washington State or a Portuguese Vinta Verde.

What Else to Take

- Wineglasses
- Cloth napkins
- Ground cloth
- Old quilt
- Insect repellent

Crostini

*A Tuscan standby, crostini are typically served with pâté
or tapenade (olive spread) in Italy.*

1 baguette†

olive oil

1 clove of garlic

pâté or roasted red pepper
  spread

† A french bread that's been formed into
a long, narrow cylinder-shaped loaf.

1. Preheat oven or toaster oven to 350°F.

2. Thinly slice the baguette and brush or spray olive oil on both sides.

3. Toast the slices until golden brown on both sides.

4. Remove from oven and rub garlic clove onto both sides of toast.

5. Bring to the picnic in a plastic bag. To serve, spread with your favorite spread and serve immediately.

8 servings

Gourmet shops usually have a wonderful selection of spreads to enjoy on crostini. Besides the traditional pâté or tapenade, I suggest a roasted red pepper spread. I also love it with a creamy, tangy goat cheese.

Tortellini Chicken Salad

This is such a delicious salad that the recipe is for eight servings even though we assume only two will go on this romantic picnic. You will have no trouble using up the remaining salad. The alternative is to cut the recipe in half and save the rest for lunch.

---

6 chicken breast halves

2 tablespoons olive oil

2 clove of garlic, minced

9 ounces fresh tortellini pasta

3 stalks of celery, sliced

1 medium purple onion, chopped

1 medium green bell pepper, seeded and chopped

¼ pound smoked Gruyère cheese, cut into ½-inch cubes

½ teaspoon salt

freshly ground black pepper

VINAIGRETTE

¾ cup cider vinegar

¼ cup honey

2 tablespoons Dijon mustard

1 teaspoon dry mustard

¾ cup corn oil

1. Place the chicken breasts in a large pot and barely cover with cold water. Bring the water to a boil over high heat. Reduce the heat and simmer the chicken for 20 minutes, or until it is just cooked through. Let the chicken cool slightly in the liquid.

2. When the chicken can be handled, remove the meat from the bones and cut into ½- by 3-inch strips.

3. Heat the olive oil in a large skillet, add the garlic, and sauté until golden brown. Remove the garlic and reserve. Add the chicken to the skillet and sauté for 1 minute, stirring constantly.

4. Cook the tortellini in a large pot of boiling water according to the directions on the package. Drain and rinse quickly in cold water.

5. Toss the chicken, reserved garlic, tortellini, celery, onion, green pepper, Gruyère, salt, and pepper to taste in a large bowl.

6. TO MAKE THE VINAIGRETTE, put the vinegar, honey, and both mustards into a blender or food processor and process until blended. While the motor is running, slowly drizzle in the oil and blend until creamy. Pour over the salad and stir well.

7. Pack two cups of the salad in a covered container and chill in the refrigerator until it is time to pack the cooler. Cover the remaining salad and serve to family or friends.

Serves 8

Citrus Salad

*A quick and easy salad that is easy to multiply.
I love the colors of this salad and its refreshing flavor.*

---

4 leaves red leaf lettuce,
  washed, dried, and crisped

½ small purple onion, thinly
  sliced

1 grapefruit half, peeled and
  sectioned

1 orange, peeled and
  sectioned

MUSTARD VINAIGRETTE

2 tablespoons Dijon mustard

1 tablespoon white wine
  vinegar

1 teaspoon sugar

1 clove of garlic, minced

¼ teaspoon salt

freshly ground black pepper

⅓ cup vegetable oil

1. Chill the lettuce in a resealable plastic bag in the refrigerator.

2. Combine the onion and grapefruit and orange sections in a small bowl. Pack in a tightly covered container and chill in the refrigerator.

3. TO MAKE THE MUSTARD VINAIGRETTE, whisk together the mustard, vinegar, sugar, garlic, salt, and pepper to taste in a small bowl. Slowly whisk in the oil until the mixture is creamy. Pour the vinaigrette into a small jar with a tight-fitting lid and take to the picnic.

4. To serve the salad, place some lettuce leaves on each plate, then a serving of the salad; top with the vinaigrette.

Serves 2

Preparing Orange Sections

To peel oranges and grapefruit, cut off the skin in one long spiral starting from the top. To make sections, hold the fruit over a bowl and, with a paring knife, slice between fruit and membrane, turn the knife under the section and up the other side. Repeat until all sections are cut from the membrane. Squeeze the juice from the membrane and drink it as your reward for a job well done.

Blueberry Muffins

Here is my version of this old-time favorite. Blueberries are not only tasty, they are healthful and keep well. Add them to cereal, pancakes, yogurt, or other berries, pour them over ice cream or pudding, or just enjoy them right out of the container..

1⅔ cups all-purpose flour
¾ cup sugar
⅓ cup wheat germ
1 teaspoon baking soda
½ teaspoon salt
1½ cups blueberries
    (preferably small
    wild ones)
1 cup buttermilk
2 tablespoons butter, melted
sweet butter to spread on
    the muffins

1. Preheat oven to 400°F. Grease 12 muffin-pan cups.

2. In a large bowl, combine the flour, sugar, wheat germ, baking soda, and salt. Add the blueberries and stir to coat the berries. Add the buttermilk and butter and stir until just combined.

3. Spoon the batter into the prepared pan and bake for 18 minutes, or until golden brown. Cool in the pan for 2 minutes. Remove from the pan and cool completely on a wire rack.

4. Pack four of the muffins in a plastic bag for the picnic. Pack a small container of sweet butter to serve with them.

Makes 12 muffins

When blueberries are in season, I either buy or pick lots and freeze them unwashed for use throughout the year. When ready to use, quickly rinse them off and dry them on paper towels.

Lemon Sand Torte
with Fruit

This rich, old-fashioned German cake recipe comes from a friend of my grandmother's and was another regular on the kaffeeklatsch table.

───────────

2 cups (4 sticks) butter, softened

1¼ cups sugar

2 cups all-purpose flour

1 teaspoon baking powder

5 eggs

2 tablespoons grated lemon zest

1 quart fresh strawberries

1. Preheat oven to 350°F. Grease and flour a tube pan.

2. In the large bowl of an electric mixer, cream the butter and sugar until light and fluffy.

3. In a small bowl, combine the flour and baking powder.

4. With the mixer at low speed, add the eggs to the butter mixture, one at a time, beating after each addition. Add some of the flour mixture after each egg until all the eggs and all the flour are in the batter. Add the lemon zest and continue beating for 1 minute.

5. Pour the batter into the prepared pan and bake for 1 hour, or until golden brown on top and a tester inserted in the cake comes out clean.

6. Cool the cake for 10 minutes on a wire rack. Remove from the pan and continue cooling on a wire rack. When cool, slice the cake and arrange some of the slices on a picnic plate. Cover with plastic wrap, then pack in the picnic basket when you are ready to go. Cover the remaining cake and enjoy at another time. You may also double wrap the remaining cake and store in the freezer.

7. Rinse the strawberries and leave the hulls on. Place them in a resealable plastic bag and pack in the cooler. Serve them alongside the cake.

Serves 8

Reunion on an Island Picnic

Menu

Gazpacho madrileño*

———

Barbecued butterflied lamb*

———

Cold rice salad*
and cucumber raita*

———

Carrots with minted
mustard vinaigrette*

———

Sourdough rye bread
and sweet butter

———

Assorted fresh fruits
and strawberry cookies*

———

Lemon ice water
or California wines

*Recipe included in this chapter

O ne of my fond memories of living in the San Francisco Bay area is of gathering together all the hometown friends we could find and taking a ferry to Angel Island in San Francisco Bay for a picnic. Recipes were handed out in advance, and everyone contributed an essential ingredient to a wonderful afternoon by the sparkling waters of the bay. Find an island and gather old friends together.

Wine Suggestions

Try a fine Bordeaux or California Cabernet Sauvignon or a merlot or a Guigal Côtes du Rhone.

What Else to Take

For the Food

- Good carving knife
- Platter
- Cups for soup
- Corkscrew
- Wineglasses
- A bowl for the fruit
- Hibachi, unless there is a grill
- Charcoal and matches

Extras

- Tablecloth
- Cloth napkins
- Flowers

Gazpacho Madrileño

A cold Spanish soup made from garden fresh vegetables whets the appetite for what is to follow. My sister-in-law brought this recipe to me from her years in Madrid. It is the essence of cool and refreshing.

---

1 medium cucumber, peeled, seeded,† and cut into quarters

1 small green bell pepper, seeded and cut into chunks

1 clove of garlic

3 medium-large tomatoes, seeded and cut into chunks

2 tablespoons red wine vinegar

¼ teaspoon ground cumin

½ teaspoon salt

5 tablespoons olive oil

3 cups water

GARNISHES

1 small cucumber, peeled, seeded,† and chopped

1 small green bell pepper, seeded and chopped

1 small tomato, seeded and chopped

† If cucumber seeds are small, leave them be.

1. Place the cucumber, pepper, and garlic in a blender or food processor and process briefly. Add the tomatoes, vinegar, cumin, and salt and blend until smooth.

2. With the motor running, gradually drizzle the oil into the mixture and blend until creamy. You have made a concentrate, which you can store in the refrigerator.

3. Add the water and pour the soup into a 1½-quart covered container. Pack in the picnic cooler.

4. Place the garnishes in small individual covered containers and chill until ready to go. Serve the soup in cups and let people choose which garnishes they want.

Serves 8

Barbecued Butterflied Lamb

This civilized way to cook a leg of lamb comes from A Private Collection
*by the Junior League of Palo Alto, California. On one memorable biking picnic,
also in California, the entire lamb was splayed on a huge grill placed over an
enormous fire. The marinade was applied with a mop. While that was
dramatic and fun, this is more manageable and tastier.*

one 6- to 7-pound leg of lamb,
    butterflied

  1 cup dry red wine

 ¾ cup beef broth

  3 tablespoons orange
    marmalade

  2 tablespoons red wine
    vinegar

  1 tablespoon dried marjoram

  1 tablespoon dried rosemary

  1 tablespoon minced dried
    onion

  1 teaspoon salt

 ¼ teaspoon ground ginger

  1 large bay leaf, crumbled

  1 clove of garlic, minced

1. Put the lamb in a shallow roasting pan, fat side down.

2. Combine the remaining ingredients in a large saucepan over medium heat. Simmer, uncovered, for 20 minutes. Pour the hot mixture over the lamb, cover, and let sit for 6 to 8 hours in the refrigerator to marinate. Remove the lamb from the refrigerator no more than 1 hour before cooking. (This can be the time spent traveling to the picnic site.)

3. Prepare a charcoal fire of medium-hot coals. Place the lamb on the grill and cook for 30 to 45 minutes. Turn the meat several times, being careful not to pierce it. Brush the lamb with the marinade as it is cooking.

4. Place the lamb on a platter and slice it thinly on a slight diagonal. Arrange the slices on a plate and put onto the picnic table.

Serves 8

Cold Rice Salad

This easily expanded salad, which is great for a crowd, is a nice alternative to the usual cold salads. People love the spicy flavors and crunchy texture.

---

6 cups cooked brown rice
¾ cup dried currants
½ cup toasted slivered almonds
1 Granny Smith or other tart apple, cored and chopped
1 medium purple onion, thinly sliced
1 medium green bell pepper, seeded and chopped
¼ cup capers
½ teaspoon peeled and grated fresh ginger root

DRESSING
½ cup white wine vinegar
1 tablespoon sugar
2 teaspoons curry powder
1 teaspoon dry mustard
½ teaspoon ground cardamom
½ teaspoon ground mace
½ teaspoon salt
¼ teaspoon ground cinnamon
¼ teaspoon cayenne pepper
freshly ground black pepper
¾ cup vegetable oil

1. In a large bowl, mix together the rice, currants, almonds, apple, onion, pepper, capers, and ginger root.

2. TO MAKE THE DRESSING, place all of the ingredients except the oil in a blender or food processor and process until blended. With the machine running, slowly drizzle in the oil until the mixture creamy.

3. Pour the dressing over the salad and chill for several hours. Pack the salad in a 2-quart covered container to transport to the picnic. This salad can be served at room or "air" temperature.

Serves 8

Cucumber Raita

*This cool Indian yogurt salad is the perfect foil for hot spicy dishes.
I love it with the rice salad.*

---

2 slicing cucumbers, peeled, seeded, and grated or chopped

1 cup plain nonfat yogurt

1 teaspoon chopped fresh mint leaves

¼ teaspoon ground cumin

1. Press the cucumbers through a strainer to remove some of the water.

2. Combine with other ingredients and take to the picnic in a small covered dish.

Makes 1½ cups

While cucumbers are commonly found in raita, other vegetables or fruits can be used. Try grated eggplant, potato, or chopped spinach. How about a banana or mango raita? Increase the spicy flavor by adding garam masala, a spicy, aromatic Indian blend of peppercorns, cardamom, cinnamon, cloves, coriander, nutmeg, turmeric, and fennel seeds available in gourmet or natural foods stores. You can also replace the curry powder in Cold Rice Salad (opposite page) with garam masala.

Carrots
with Minted Mustard Vinaigrette

Turn plain old carrots into fancy with a hint of mint and a touch of piquant. Raw carrot sticks can be boring, but cook these colorful roots, then glaze them, caramelize them, or add a vibrant dressing and you'll have a fantastic side dish.

---

6 large carrots, peeled and sliced ⅛-inch thick

¼ cup chopped fresh mint leaves

MUSTARD VINAIGRETTE

¼ cup lemon vinegar or lemon juice

2 tablespoons olive oil

2 tablespoons vegetable oil

1 tablespoon Dijon mustard

¼ teaspoon white pepper

¼ teaspoon salt

1. Steam the carrots for 10 minutes or until tender crisp, or cook them in a microwave oven for 5 to 8 minutes until tender crisp.

2. TO MAKE THE MUSTARD VINAIGRETTE, mix the hot carrots in a bowl with the vinegar, oils, mustard, pepper, and salt. Cover the bowl and cool in the refrigerator for about 30 minutes.

3. Sprinkle the mint onto the cooled carrots and pack in a covered container to take to the picnic. These carrots are best served at "air" temperature.

Serves 8

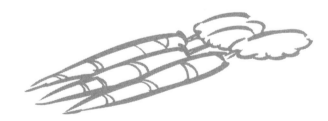

Strawberry Cookies

To make these whimsical cookies, you will need a strawberry-shaped cookie cutter. Without the strawberry-shaped cutter, you will have a tender, lemon-flavored sugar cookie in the shape of your choice.

¾   cup sugar
½   cup solid shortening
¼   cup milk
1   egg, lightly beaten
2   teaspoons grated lemon zest
1   teaspoon almond extract
2½   cups unsifted all-purpose flour
2   teaspoons baking powder
red and green food coloring

❈❈❈❈❈❈❈❈❈

Tint yellow dough and cut rounds for lemon slices. Pipe with yellow-tinted lemon icing (see page 148 from Teddy Bear Picnic) to resemble lemon slices.

1. In the large bowl of an electric mixer, cream the sugar and shortening at medium speed until light and fluffy. Beat in the milk, egg, lemon zest, and almond extract until well blended.

2. Sift together the flour and baking powder into a medium-sized bowl and gradually add to the creamed mixture until the dough is well mixed.

3. Wrap the dough in plastic wrap. Chill for 1 hour, or until firm.

4. Preheat oven to 350°F.

5. Divide the dough in half, form each half into a flattened ball, and place one on a lightly floured surface. Roll the dough to ⅛-inch thickness. Using the strawberry cutter, cut out the cookies and place them on ungreased baking sheets. With a skewer, make small indentations on the cookies to resemble strawberry seeds. Put 1 tablespoon of water in each of two small dishes and add a few drops of food coloring to each. Brush the stems of the cookies lightly with the green food coloring and the fruit with the red.

6. Bake the cookies for 8 minutes, or until lightly browned around the edges. Remove from the baking sheets and cool on wire racks. Repeat with the second ball of dough. To save time, you might make only a special few with the strawberry cutter and the remaining ones the shape of your choice.

Makes 5 dozen

Moonlight on a Mountaintop Picnic

On a mountaintop, bright moonlight casts a glow of romance and wonder. Food may not be necessary, but for hungry lovers, here is a romantic menu. Pack the food in attractive little containers, don't take too much, and put it all in an old-fashioned romantic picnic basket. Choose a mountain that is easy to reach on foot.

Wine Suggestions

Try a California Pinot Noir or a slightly chilled Chinon or Bourgueil from France.

What Else to Take

- Wineglasses
- A flashlight, in case the moonlight fails
- Blanket or ground cover
- Flowers
- Cloth napkins

Menu

Thai grilled shrimp appetizer* with crackers

———

Roast beef salad*

———

Crusty French bread with pesto butter*

———

Sliced tomatoes with lemon caper sauce*

———

Chocolate-dipped strawberries*

———

Red wine

*Recipe included in this chapter

Thai Grilled Shrimp Appetizer

*Lemon grass is a wonder of southeast Asian cuisine. The tough stalk,
when pulled away, releases a light, lemony fragrance that perfumes many
a delicate dish. Here it lends its mystery to a spicy marinade.*

8 large shrimp with tails,
about ½ pound

3 tablespoons rice vinegar

¼ teaspoon crushed red
pepper flakes

1-inch piece fresh lemon
grass

2 tablespoons peanut oil

1 tablespoon chopped
cilantro

1 teaspoon fresh minced
ginger root

1 clove of garlic, crushed

two 8-inch bamboo skewers
soaked in water

1. Rinse shrimp and place in a shallow bowl.

2. In a small bowl, mix the vinegar and pepper flakes.
Peel the tough outer layer from the lemon grass to reveal the
fragrant center. Chop and add to the mix with the remaining ingredients. Pour over the shrimp and marinate in the
refrigerator for 30 minutes.

3. Prepare a small fire on a grill or hibachi. Thread the
shrimp onto the skewers and grill for 2 minutes per side, or
until the shrimp turn pink and white. Cool and store in the
refrigerator in plastic bags until ready to pack into the cooler
for the picnic.

Serves 2

Roast Beef Salad

*Plan to grill the beef before making this delightfully zesty salad.
Grill it before grilling the shrimp for the appetizer.*

---

2 cups cold cooked, London
  broil or flank steak, thinly
  sliced and julienned

⅓ cup balsamic vinegar

3 sun-dried tomatoes,
  julienned

1 tablespoon olive oil

1 tablespoon sesame oil

1 teaspoon horseradish

salt and freshly ground black
  pepper

1. Mix all of the ingredients in a large bowl.
2. Place in a covered container and chill until time to pack it in your insulated bag.

Serves 2

To prepare for this salad, grill a 3-pound London broil or flank steak over a hot fire for about 5 minutes per side, or until cooked but still rare. Thinly slice on the diagonal; be sure to save enough for the salad. Let the grill cool, then clean the grate with a wire brush.

Crusty French Bread
with Pesto Butter

Flavoring the butter with pesto gives an unbeatable fragrance to a crusty loaf.

½ cup (1 stick) sweet butter, softened

¼ cup Piquant Pesto

1 loaf fresh crusty French bread

1. Preheat oven to 350°F.
2. Mix the butter and pesto in a small bowl.
3. Slice the bread lengthwise; spread the butter on one cut side.
4. Wrap the bread in aluminum foil and place in the oven for 15 minutes just before leaving for the picnic.
5. Wrap the warm loaf in a tablecloth and pack it in your picnic basket. Break off hunks of bread to eat with the roast beef salad.

Serves 2 or more

Piquant Pesto

Pesto bursts with summer. Traditionally it is chopped basil, smoothed out with olive oil, Parmesan cheese, and pine nuts. Try parsley and/or walnuts instead.

2 cups fresh basil leaves

6 large cloves of garlic

1 cup pine nuts

1 cup olive oil

1 cup Parmesan cheese, freshly grated

salt and freshly ground black pepper

1. In a food processor, process the basil, garlic, and nuts.
2. With the machine running, pour the olive oil into the processor in a slow steady stream.
3. Add the cheese and salt and pepper to taste and process briefly.

Makes 2 cups

Sliced Tomatoes
with Lemon Caper Sauce

For an elegant touch, dab a little sauce onto these luscious sliced garden-fresh tomatoes.

---

2 fresh ripe tomatoes

LEMON CAPER SAUCE
  2 tablespoons mayonnaise
  2 tablespoons plain nonfat yogurt
  1 tablespoon drained capers
  1 tablespoon lemon juice
  1 teaspooon grated lemon zest

1. Bring a quart of water to a boil. Immerse tomatoes for 30 seconds. Remove from water with a fork and peel. The skin will easily come off. Remove stem; core and slice. Arrange in a shallow plastic container.

2. TO MAKE THE LEMON CAPER SAUCE, combine the remaining ingredients in a small bowl and gently whisk. Pour into a small jar and take to the picnic with the tomatoes.

Serves 2

My favorite tool for grating lemon zest is a microplane grater that looks like it belongs in a workshop more than in a kitchen. A long narrow grater blade is set in a handle. To use, run the blade lightly along the surface of the lemon, turning the fruit as you move the blade back and forth. Before long, you will have a pile of light and fluffy zest with none of the bitter underlying white pith. This tool produces an equally fine result when grating any hard cheese.

Chocolate-Dipped Strawberries

*Strawberries keep best if they are unwashed and have their stems on.
For these luscious dipped strawberries, keep the green hulls on also.*

---

1 cup semisweet chocolate chips, melted†

3 tablespoons Grand Marnier liqueur

2 tablespoons butter, melted

¼ cup confectioners' sugar

1 tablespoon water

selected large fresh strawberries

†Don't let the chocolate get hot; around 110°F is perfect. A microwave oven is useful for this step.

1. Combine the chocolate, Grand Marnier, and butter in a small bowl and whisk together.

2. Add the confectioners' sugar and water and continue whisking until smooth.

3. Just before dipping berries, rinse them and gently pat them dry with paper towels. Lay a piece of wax paper on a work surface.

4. Dip the strawberries about three-quarters of the way into the chocolate. Let them drain on the wax paper and sit until the chocolate has set. Pack them carefully in a small lidded tin, lined with wax paper. They don't keep for long — make them the day you plan to have your picnic.

Makes 1 cup

Strawberries can absorb water if washed and then stored in the refrigerator. They remain fresher with the hulls on, too!

AUTUMN OUTINGS

*A*utumn is the precious, fleeting season between the languid, sun-filled days of summer and the cold, short days of winter. Nature provides us with a blaze of color for this final fling of outdoor living. In New England, the best days for viewing fall color are slightly overcast, the vivid colors standing out in stark contrast to the gray sky. But the best days for picnics are the clear, warm days of Indian summer that bring us outside for hikes, soccer games, tailgating at football games, or just walking in the neighborhood.

Picnics

AUTUMN DAY-HIKE PICNIC

———

SPORTS-FAN PICNIC

———

FRIENDS ON A
MOUNTAINSIDE PICNIC

———

TAILGATE PICNIC

———

AUTUMN BEACH PICNIC

———

TEDDY BEAR'S BIRTHDAY
PARTY PICNIC

———

WINE-COUNTRY PICNIC

Autumn Day-Hike Picnic

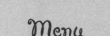

Menu

This menu is for a warm fall day. If the weather is cool, heat the soup and pour it into hot thermos bottles.

Iced borscht*

Thinly sliced Danish ham with boursin*

Garden lettuce

Zesty rye bread*

Bodil's almond tart* with ruby red grapes

Cider

*Recipe included in this chapter

As a New Englander, I am well aware of the appeal of this time of year, when the air is golden, country roads are brilliant, and mountainsides are muted. New Englanders are driven to spend as many hours in the crisp, clear air as possible before the winter winds sweep down. Even raking leaves offers enjoyment, because it is an opportunity to be outdoors. But more fun is crunching through fallen leaves on a winding trail in search of a sunny spot by a stream. It is a bittersweet time of year, so beautiful and so fleeting that one should enjoy every golden moment of it. Pack a picnic and take a hike.

What Else to Take

- Gorp
- Backpacks
- Small insulated bag with ice pack
- Space blanket
- Lots of water
- Garbage bag for trash

Plan Your Packing

With fresh air and exercise, hikers will be hungry. One deserves to eat heartily after vigorous exercise. Be generous but not excessive with the food. Use lightweight food containers and take several packs — one for cold items, one for hot, one for food that doesn't need either cold or hot, and one for the nonfood items. Be sure everyone gets to carry a pack and has their own water bottle. Don't leave any trash in the woods.

Iced Borscht

*The jewel-like color of this soup is spectacular. For a hot soup
with an intense, rich look and flavor, leave out the buttermilk. Buttermilk
smooths the texture, resulting in a gorgeous, creamy, cold soup.*

---

1 quart water

8 small to medium beets, cut
   into quarters

1 tablespoon butter

1 tablespoon corn oil

1 medium onion, chopped

1 clove of garlic, minced

3 cups chicken stock

1 tablespoon chopped fresh
   dill

1 tablespoon lemon juice

½ teaspoon salt

¼ teaspoon white pepper

2 cups buttermilk

¼ cup sour cream mixed with
   ¼ cup plain yogurt for
   topping

   dill sprigs for garnish

1. Bring the water to a boil in a large saucepan. Add the beets and cook them for about 30 minutes, or until tender when pierced with a fork. Drain and rinse the beets in cold water. When cool enough to handle, slip the skins off.

2. Heat the butter and oil in a large skillet over medium heat. Sauté the onion for 5 minutes, or until translucent. Add the garlic and cook for 1 minute, then remove from the heat. Add the chicken stock, dill, lemon juice, salt, and pepper.

3. Place some stock and some beets in a blender or food processor and purée. Pour the soup into a large bowl and repeat the processing until all of the broth and beets are puréed. Add the buttermilk, stir to blend, and chill for several hours.

4. Pour the soup into cold thermos bottles and place an ice cube in each one.

5. Pack the sour cream mixture in a small covered container and place it in the cooler for traveling. The dill sprigs can be transported in a resealable plastic bag. At serving time, pour the soup into attractive cups, top each serving with a tablespoon of the sour cream mixture, and garnish with a dill sprig.

Serves 8

• *For attractive "fall color" borscht, use golden beets.*

• *Omit the buttermilk and serve hot with a dollop of sour cream.*

Boursin

Not designed for those watching their cholesterol. However, since this is so good, the trick is to eat a small amount of it. A thin layer on a slice of bread provides a wonderful background for the ham.

---

8 ounces cream cheese, softened

½ cup (1 stick) butter, softened

1 tablespoon lemon juice

1 tablespoon minced fresh chives

1 tablespoon minced fresh parsley

1 teaspoon dried tarragon

½ teaspoon dry mustard

½ teaspoon Worcestershire sauce

1 clove of garlic, minced

1. Place all of the ingredients in a food processor and process until well mixed. Refrigerate the cheese for 3 days to blend the flavors.

2. Place in a 1-pint covered container and refrigerate until ready to pack the picnic.

Makes 1½ cups

Fresh Herbs vs. Dry

Many herbs, such as oregano, sage, and tarragon, maintain their fragrance when dried. Parsley does not. Fortunately, fresh parsley is always available. If you grow your own parsley, I suggest washing, drying, and mincing some, then freezing it in small resealable bags. You can do the same with chives. I prefer frozen chopped basil and cilantro to the dried as well.

Note: If you substitute fresh herbs for dried in a recipe, remember to use at least twice as much.

Zesty Rye Bread

A very tasty loaf that is quite dense and can be thinly sliced with ease. The orange and fennel combine subtly with the richness of the bread for outstanding flavor.

1½   cups warm (110°F) water

2   tablespoons active dry yeast

¼   cup molasses

¼   cup fresh orange juice

2   tablespoons butter, softened

2   tablespoons grated orange zest

4   teaspoons anise seeds

4   teaspoons fennel seeds

1   tablespoon sugar

½   teaspoon crushed cardamom seeds

2½   cups rye flour

1   teaspoon salt

1½ to 2   cups all-purpose flour

1. Sprinkle the yeast over the warm water in a large bowl and let sit about 5 minutes, or until the yeast is dissolved. Mix the molasses, orange juice, butter, orange zest, anise, fennel, sugar, and cardamom seeds together in a small bowl.

2. When the yeast is dissolved, add the molasses mixture to the yeast and stir to blend.

3. Add the rye flour and the salt and beat with a whisk until the flour is well blended. Gradually add the all-purpose flour, 1 cup at a time, and beat it with a wooden spoon. When the dough seems to come together in a ball in the center of the bowl and is soft but not sticky, scrape the sides of the bowl and dump all the contents onto a lightly floured surface. At this point, you will not have added the total amount of the all-purpose flour.

4. Knead the dough for about 10 minutes. As it gets sticky, add small amounts of the remaining all-purpose flour. When the dough is well kneaded, it will have absorbed most of the flour and will be smooth and round and softly firm to the touch. It should not be sticky (too little flour) or rigid (too much flour).

RECIPE CONTINUES ON NEXT PAGE

Double the recipe, freeze extra loaves double-wrapped in plastic, and give them as gifts.

5. Put the dough into a clean, oiled bowl, turn the dough over to coat it with oil, cover it with a damp towel, and let it rise in a warm, draft-free place until it is double in size, 45 minutes to 1 hour.

6. Grease a baking sheet. When the dough has doubled in size, punch it down and knead it two times to form a smooth shape and to release the air bubbles. Divide the dough into two equal pieces and shape each half into a smooth oval. Place the loaves on the baking sheet and let them rise for 1 hour.

7. Preheat oven to 350°F.

8. Before baking, make three diagonal slashes across the top of each loaf. Bake for 30 minutes. Remove from the baking sheet and cool on a wire rack. When the bread is cool, store it in plastic bags. Slice the loaves before packing the picnic.

Makes 3 small round loaves

Gorp

I enjoy backpacking, but I love gorp. Gorp used to be just "good old raisins and peanuts." You can doll up this favorite hiking snack by adding dried cranberries or cherries, filberts or macadamia nuts, sunflower seeds, and tropical fruit bits. Dried cereal or popcorn can be mixed in for body without bulk, and for extra impetus to make it to the summit, there's the universal favorite — chocolate — in chips or chunks or m&ms®.

Bodil's Almond Tart

Bodil, who is Danish and a wonderful cook, shared this recipe with me. It has been to many picnics ever since. This delightful tart can be made quickly and packs beautifully. While you're at it, you can make two and freeze one for another picnic.

CRUST

    1 *cup all-purpose flour*

    6 *tablespoons butter*

    3 *tablespoons*
        confectioners' sugar

FILLING

    ½ *cup sugar*

    ¼ *cup butter*

    2 *eggs*

1 to 2 *teaspoons almond extract*

    1 *cup chopped almonds*

1. Preheat oven to 350°F.

2. TO MAKE THE CRUST, place the flour, butter, and confectioners' sugar in a food processor. Process the mixture until it has a crumbly appearance. Pour the crumbly mixture into a 10-inch tart pan and press it against the bottom and sides to create a uniform crust.

3. TO MAKE THE FILLING, cream the sugar and butter until fluffy in the large bowl of an electric mixer. Add the eggs and almond extract and continue beating until well combined. At low speed, add the almonds and mix just until blended.

4. Pour the filling into the crust and bake for 20 minutes, or until the filling is set and slightly darkened. Cool in the pan on a wire rack. When the tart is cool, slice it into eight pieces and carefully wrap two pieces at a time in aluminum foil. If you make the tart well in advance, these packages can be frozen until it is time to pack the picnic.

Serves 8

Sports-Fan Picnic

Menu

Corn chowder*

Fruit salsa* and chips

Picnic calzones*

Mediterranean torte*

Huge tossed salad*

Rice and peanut
crispy bars*

Bowl of fresh fruit

Assorted bottled waters,
seltzer, and juice

*Recipe included in this chapter

Whether it's a beautiful fall afternoon or a gray drizzly day, cheering family members at soccer or football games or cross-country meets leaves you with indelible images of autumn sport. After the game, gather the team and fans to celebrate at a potluck picnic. These recipes are sure to please; each serves eight people, so plan accordingly.

What Else to Take

- Bags of corn chips
- Foam cups for soup
- Plastic tablecloth

Potluck Pleasures

Frequently, when friends, family, or fans gather for a picnic, the meal is orchestrated around a special event, in this case a sporting event. Potluck picnics are easy because everyone contributes to the meal. Potluck picnics can be completely random with participants bringing a recipe of their choice, highly organized with the planner handing out specific recipes, or somewhere in between. I rather like the completely random approach when people bring their favorite foods. One runs the risk of having all desserts, but that wouldn't be so bad, would it?

Corn Chowder

A perfect soup for fall that makes excellent use of the harvest's end, corn chowder is one of my favorites. With a slice of bread and a steaming bowl of chowder, you have all you need for a hearty lunch.

---

4 slices bacon

1 medium onion, minced

4 medium potatoes, peeled and diced

2 cups water or chicken stock

3 cups corn kernels

4 cups scalded milk†

3 tablespoons butter

salt and freshly ground black pepper

2 cups grated Cheddar cheese (optional)

†For a richer chowder, substitute 1 cup heavy cream for 1 cup of milk. For a low-calorie soup, use skim milk.

1. Place the bacon in a large kettle or Dutch oven with a cover. Cook the bacon until evenly browned. Remove the bacon from the pan and set aside. Pour off all but 1 tablespoon of the bacon fat.

2. Add the onion to the kettle and cook about 5 minutes or until slightly browned. Add the potatoes and water or stock, bring to a boil, and simmer for 10 to 15 minutes, or until the potatoes are soft.

3. Add the corn and milk and heat thoroughly, but do not boil. Add the butter and the salt and pepper to taste. Pour the chowder into two wide-mouth thermos bottles and place in the pack. Crumble the bacon and place it in a seal-lock plastic bag. Place the cheese in another seal-lock plastic bag. After serving the soup, garnish each cup with some bacon and ¼ cup cheese.

Serves 8

To add more color and flavor, add chopped red and green peppers to the onions when sautéing.

Fruit Salsa

*The sweet and tart combination provides a refreshing background
for grilled chicken as well as a tasty accompaniment for chips.*

½ ripe mango
½ ripe avocado
2 tablespoons fresh lime juice
1 nectarine, peeled and cut
   into ¼-inch dice
½ cup chopped red onion
½ cup fresh cantaloupe, cut
   into ¼-inch dice
2 tomatillos, with paperlike
   skin removed, and cut into
   ¼-inch dice
2 tablespoons fresh cilantro
½ teaspoon minced jalapeño

1. With a fork, mash the mango and avocado together in a medium bowl. Blend in the lime juice.

2. Stir in the remaining ingredients until well mixed. Pack in a resealable container. Serve with corn chips as an appetizer.

Makes about 3 cups

Tomatillos are also known as Mexican green tomatoes. Remove the paperlike outer husk to reveal a firm, crisp flesh with a tart, lemon flavor that adds both texture and taste to salsas.

Picnic Calzones

*These pastries could be called pocket pizzas. Start with a simple yeast dough,
fill it with your favorite pizza filling, and wrap it up in a neat little package.*

---

1 cup warm (110°F)
  water

1 tablespoon active dry
  yeast

1 tablespoon honey

½ teaspoon salt

2½ to 3 cups all-purpose flour

FILLING

Fill the calzones with whatever you love! Here are some suggestions that you can use in combination to equal 1 cup of filling.

- One 10-ounce package frozen spinach, steamed and well drained
- Ricotta cheese
- Grated mozzarella cheese
- Grated Parmesan cheese
- Sautéed chopped onions and garlic
- Tomato sauce

---

1. In a large bowl, place the water, yeast, honey, and salt. Stir with a wooden spoon until the yeast has dissolved.

2. Add 2 cups of the flour and beat the mixture with the wooden spoon until it is smooth. Gradually add the remaining flour and continue to stir with the wooden spoon, until the dough forms a ball.

3. Scrape the dough out of the bowl and place it on a lightly floured surface and knead the dough until it is smooth and elastic. Add more flour if the dough becomes sticky.

4. Place the dough in a lightly greased bowl and cover it with a damp towel. Let the dough rise in a warm spot for 1 hour, or until double in bulk. Punch down the dough. At this point, it is ready to be shaped. If that is not possible, store in the freezer.

5. Preheat oven to 450°F.

6. Divide the dough into 8 equal parts. Roll each piece into a ¼-inch-thick round that is about 5 inches in diameter. With a finger, moisten one-half inch around the edge of each piece with water.

7. Place 2 to 3 tablespoons of filling on each round, slightly off-center. Fold the empty side over the filling and crimp with a fork. Prick holes in the top.

8. Bake on an ungreased baking sheet for 15 to 20 minutes, or until lightly browned.

Serves 8

Mediterranean Torte

A spectacular dish to set before friends, fans, and teens. This creation from Chef Irene Maston is easy to make and filled with the much-loved flavors of Italy.

1½ pounds bread dough (frozen store-bought dough, your favorite bread dough recipe, or use the recipe from Picnic Calzones, page 125)

8 ounces genoa salami, arranged in two 4-ounce stacks

1 quart cleaned whole small mushrooms

1 cup drained and dried black olives

8 ounces provolone, arranged in two 4-ounce stacks

8 ounces thinly sliced ham arranged in two 4-ounce stacks

1½ pounds frozen chopped spinach, thawed and squeezed dry

one 13¾-ounce can pimientos, drained and dried

1½ cups drained and dried artichoke quarters

1 egg yolk mixed with 1 tablespoon water

1. Preheat oven to 350°F.

2. Use one quarter of the dough to roll out a 10-inch circle for the top. Set this piece aside.

3. Roll out the rest of the dough so it fills a 10-inch springform pan, with one inch of dough hanging over the edge. Arrange the filling in the following order from bottom to top, spreading each ingredient in a layer on top of the preceding one: 4 ounces of the salami, mushrooms, olives, 4 ounces of the provolone, 4 ounces of the ham, spinach, pimientos, remaining 4 ounces of salami.

4. Fold the excess dough in over the filling and continue layering with the remaining 4 ounces of ham, ½ inch from the edge, artichokes, and remaining 4 ounces of provolone.

5. Brush the edge of the dough with the egg glaze and place the top piece of dough on the edge. Brush the top with the glaze, prick a few times with a fork, and let the dough rise briefly. Bake for 45 minutes or until golden brown. Let the torte cool in the pan. Remove the sides and serve at room temperature. With a serrated knife, cut into one- to two-inch wedges before wrapping it for the picnic. Store in the refrigerator.

Serves 8

Before removing from oven, test for doneness by poking the crust with a straw. If the straw comes out clean, it's done.

Huge Tossed Salad

The secret of a great tossed salad is having wonderful fresh greens that are clean, crisp, and dry. A lettuce spinner is most helpful.

---

1 large head red lettuce

1 large head green garden lettuce, or curly endive

An assortment of any or all of the following vegetables: chunks of tomatoes, thinly sliced cucumbers,

thinly sliced purple onions, drained mandarin oranges, sliced mushrooms,

artichoke hearts, sliced avocado

Mustard Vinaigrette (see page 98), or your favorite salad dressing

1. Immerse the lettuce in a sink full of cold water. Place some of the leaves in a lettuce spinner and spin dry. Drain the excess water from the spinner and repeat the process until all the lettuce is washed and dried. Place the washed lettuce in a large plastic bag and store in the refrigerator until ready to go to the picnic.

2. Bring all the salad ingredients wrapped separately and construct the salad in a large bowl at the picnic. Toss it all together and enjoy.

Serves 8

Rice and Peanut Crispy Bars

*This variation on the traditional Rice Krispies treats
is packed with tasty, healthful ingredients.*

---

vegetable oil spray

¼ cup light maple syrup or
corn syrup

2 tablespoons butter

35 regular-sized
marshmallows

5½ cups toasted rice cereal

¾ cup toasted wheat germ or
flax or a combination of
the two

1 cup peanuts

1. Spray a 9- by 13-inch baking pan with vegetable spray.

2. In a large saucepan, simmer syrup and butter over medium heat until blended. Add marshmallows and stir until completely melted, about 5 minutes.

3. Add cereal, wheat germ, and peanuts, and stir until well coated. Transfer to pan. Spray the back of a metal spoon and press the mixture into the pan. Cover and refrigerate until well set.

3. Cut into squares, place in a resealable plastic bag, and take to the party.

Makes 32 squares

Friends on a Mountainside Picnic

An autumn day with crisp air, the smell of dry leaves, and colors at full blaze stimulates all the senses. Select a mountainside that overlooks a valley, spread your blanket on a level spot, and experience the intensity of the foliage and the muted tones on the distant hillsides.

What Else to Take

- Cooler
- Bouquet of fall flowers
- Water bottles
- Ground cloth

Menu

Cold marinated flank steak*

Tabbouleh*

Cold zucchini and tomatoes*

Creamy cucumbers*

Crusty French bread and sweet butter

Carrot cake with orange cream cheese icing*

Chilled natural fruit sodas or ice cold beer

*Recipe included in this chapter

A PRIMER ON BREADS

We have come a long way from squishy loaves of white bread. Look for these types and shapes of bread:

- *Baguette:* A long, thin loaf of French bread; chewy inside with a crust that shatters
- *Batard:* Made from a dough similar to that used for the baguette; has a wide middle and pointed ends; also considered a *rustic peasant loaf*
- *Pane Toscana:* Simple unsalted bread of Tuscany; oval shape
- *Sourdough:* Tangy, sour-flavored bread that gets its taste and rise from fermented starter; comes in many shapes and sizes
- *Peasant bread:* Rough textured, coarse loaf

Marinated Flank Steak

*My college roommate, Sonnie, introduced me to flank steak years ago
as an inexpensive way to enjoy steak. I still think you can't beat the flavor,
and when cut on the bias it's as tender as can be.*

---

one *3½ pound flank steak*
⅓ *cup corn oil*
⅓ *cup tamari*
1 *teaspoon minced fresh
   ginger root*
1 *garlic clove, minced*
1 *tablespoon lime juice*
*salt and freshly ground black
   pepper*

1. Rinse the steak in cold water, pat dry, and with a sharp knife score the surface in a crisscross pattern. Place the steak in an oblong baking dish.

2. In a small bowl, mix together the oil, tamari, ginger root, garlic, and lime juice. Pour the marinade over the flank steak. Turn the steak once to coat both sides. Cover the dish and set it in the refrigerator for 1 hour. Turn the steak during that period. Let the steak and marinade sit out of the refrigerator for 30 minutes before cooking.

3. Preheat grill to high.

4. Remove the steak from the marinade and place it on the hot grill. Cook it 5 to 7 minutes on a side, depending on the desired doneness.

5. Remove cooked steak from the grill and place it on a platter. Let it sit for several minutes, and then with a large, sharp knife, thinly slice it diagonally to the cutting surface. By slicing it this way, you will get thin strips of steak that are about 1½ inches wide.

6. Arrange the slices on a picnic plate and sprinkle them lightly with salt. Grind some pepper to taste over all. Cover the plate with plastic wrap and store in the refrigerator. Pack the steak in the cooler when ready to go on the picnic.

Serves 8

Tabbouleh

Whether spelled tabbouleh *or* tabouli, *this Middle Eastern staple of fresh herbs, tomatoes, and lemon blended into crunchy bulgur wheat recalls the tastes of summer at this fall picnic.*

---

1   cup bulgur wheat

2   cups water

3   tablespoons olive oil

3   medium tomatoes, chopped and seeded

½   cup garbanzo beans, cooked, drained, and rinsed

¼   cup chopped fresh parsley

2   tablespoons chopped fresh chives

2   tablespoons chopped fresh mint leaves

2   garlic cloves, minced

     juice of 2 lemons

¼   teaspoon salt

     freshly ground black pepper

1. Place the bulgur and water in a large saucepan and bring to a boil. Turn off heat, cover the pan, and let stand for 1 hour until the bulgur has absorbed all the water.

2. Place the bulgur mixture in a large bowl and toss it with the olive oil. Cover the bowl and place it in the refrigerator for at least 1 hour.

3. Add the remaining ingredients and gently mix the salad together. Place the tabbouleh in a 1½-quart covered container and store in the refrigerator until ready to pack the picnic. The tabbouleh does not need to be packed in a cooler.

Serves 8

• *Bulgur is wheat berries with the bran removed, then steamed, dried, and ground to various degrees of coarseness. It cooks quickly as a result of this processing. Merely pour boiling water over the grain and let it sit until plump. Then fluff with a fork and add whatever you wish.*

• *Leftover tabbouleh in a pita pocket makes a terrific quick lunch.*

Cold Zucchini and Tomatoes

*This vegetable dish is almost like a relish and can be served as such.
It goes well with grilled meats and chicken.*

¼ cup olive oil

2 tablespoons vegetable oil

2 large onions, thinly sliced

3 or 4 small zucchini, sliced

1½ pounds tomatoes, seeded and cut into bite-size chunks, or one 28-ounce can Italian tomatoes

4 leaves fresh basil, chopped, or 1 tablespoon dried basil

½ teaspoon dried oregano

½ teaspoon salt

freshly ground black pepper

1. Heat the oils in a large skillet, add the onions, and cook 5 minutes over medium heat until slightly soft. Add the zucchini, cover the skillet, and cook 10 minutes longer. Uncover, add the tomatoes, basil, oregano, salt, and pepper to taste, and cook 10 minutes, stirring frequently.

2. Pour the vegetables into a covered container and chill for at least 1 hour or until very cold. Then pack it in the picnic cooler.

Serves 8

Creamy Cucumbers

I love to eat something creamy with steak. This old favorite seems to bridge the gap between the grainy tabbouleh and the tender, juicy slices of steak.

---

3 cucumbers, peeled and thinly sliced
1 tablespoon salt
1 cup plain yogurt
2 tablespoons cider vinegar
2 tablespoons mayonnaise
2 teaspoons horseradish

1. Spread out the sliced cucumbers in a low, flat baking dish. Sprinkle them with the salt. Cover the dish and chill the cucumbers for 1 hour.

2. Place the cucumbers in a colander and thoroughly rinse. Spread them out on paper towels and pat dry. Extract as much water from the cucumbers as you can. The less water in the cucumber, the creamier the consistency of the salad.

3. In a small bowl, mix the yogurt, vinegar, mayonnaise, and horseradish until well combined.

4. Place the cucumbers in a 1-quart covered container and pour the yogurt sauce over them. Stir the mixture gently to blend. Store the cucumbers in the refrigerator until you are ready to pack the picnic. Pack the cucumbers in the cooler to keep them cold.

Makes 4 cups

Carrot Cake
with Orange Cream Cheese Icing

My friend Katie introduced me to the joys of carrot cake with this recipe.
So simple and so good!

---

2   cups all-purpose flour
1½ cups sugar
2   teaspoons baking soda
½   teaspoon ground cinnamon
¾   cup vegetable oil
4   eggs, slightly beaten
1   cup chopped walnuts
½   cup raisins
4   large carrots, peeled and grated

ICING
8   ounces cream cheese, softened
6   tablespoons butter, softened
1   pound confectioners' sugar
2   tablespoons grated orange zest
1   tablespoon orange juice

1. Preheat oven to 325°F and grease a 9- by 13-inch baking pan.

2. In a large bowl, combine the flour, sugar, baking soda, and cinnamon and stir to blend. Add the oil and eggs and mix well. Stir in the walnuts, raisins, and carrots and continue stirring until the batter is well blended.

3. Place the cake batter into the prepared baking pan. Bake for 35 to 40 minutes, or until a tester inserted in the center comes out clean. Cool the cake on a wire rack until completely cool.

4. TO MAKE THE ICING, cream the cheese and butter in a medium-sized bowl. Gradually blend in the sugar until well combined. Add the orange zest and juice and mix until smooth.

5. Ice the cooled cake, cover it with plastic wrap, and store in the refrigerator until it is time to pack it in the picnic basket.

Makes 1 cake

Tailgate Picnic

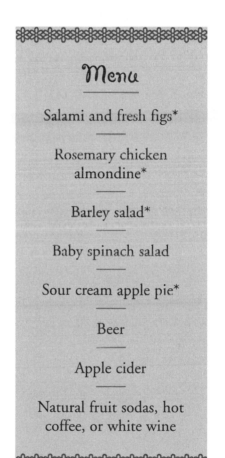

Menu

Salami and fresh figs*

Rosemary chicken almondine*

Barley salad*

Baby spinach salad

Sour cream apple pie*

Beer

Apple cider

Natural fruit sodas, hot coffee, or white wine

*Recipe included in this chapter

A beautiful early-fall Saturday, a football game, and a group of friends set the stage for a tailgate picnic. Next comes the food, and a tailgate not too far from the stadium. If not a tailgate on the back of a wagon or SUV, then a card table will do. The main thing is to be able to mingle with other tailgaters. This custom goes way back, and even nonfans get into the spirit of the game.

New England is famed for its brilliant display of color during the brief period before the leaves fly and the land becomes barren. With all the colleges in New England, many find great pleasure in packing a sumptuous feast and carting it off to their New England college game for this traditional party.

Wine Suggestions

Try a medium-bodied Petit Château from the Bordeaux Region or a California merlot or, for the adventurous, a slightly chilled Bourgueil or Chinon from the Loire Valley.

What Else to Take

- Card table
- Colorful tablecloth and napkins
- Blankets to sit on

Salami and Fresh Figs

A simple Tuscan combination bursting with a juicy sweetness that we discovered when living in Florence one fall. It is one of the traditional Tuscan combinations of meat and fruit.

---

7 *plump fresh figs*
13 *thin slices of Genoa salami*
   toothpicks

1. Wash figs and cut 6 of them into quarters.
2. Arrange 2 quarters on each of 12 of the slices of salami. Roll salami around the fig, cut in half, and place a toothpick in each cut roll.
3. On a large serving plate, place the extra piece of salami to one side. Score the skin of the remaining fig from top to widest part. Make four scoring lines. Gently peel away the skin to make petals. Cut through the fig and gently pull apart. Place fig flower on salami and arrange rolls on the plate. Cover the plate with plastic wrap and store in refrigerator, but bring to room temperature before serving. Serve and enjoy!

Makes 24 rolls to serve 8

These can be made several hours ahead without toothpicks and stored in a covered dish in the refrigerator. Serve at room temperature. Insert the toothpicks just before serving.

Rosemary Chicken Almondine

When my roommates, Kimmie and Jean, and I lived in New York, this was the specialty of the house. It has served us all well ever since, with some modifications to our contemporary palates.

——————————

4 whole boneless, skinless chicken breasts

salt and freshly ground black pepper

1 tablespoon melted butter

1 tablespoon olive oil

½ cup dry white wine

2 tablespoons chopped fresh rosemary

½ cup sliced almonds, toasted

1. Preheat oven to 350°F. Spray a shallow baking dish with vegetable cooking spray.

2. Wash the chicken and pat it dry. Arrange the chicken in a single layer in the prepared dish. Sprinkle with salt and pepper to taste.

3. Combine the butter and olive oil and pour over the chicken. Pour the wine over the chicken. Sprinkle with rosemary and scatter the almonds on top. Bake for 20 minutes, or until the chicken is cooked through. Cool slightly then arrange on a platter and cover with plastic wrap; store in the refrigerator until party time. Serve at room temperature.

Serves 8

To toast almonds, spread them thinly in the pan of a toaster oven. Turn it on to 400°F and cook for 5 to 10 minutes, or until the almonds are lightly browned and fragrant. Check them after 5 minutes, so they don't get too dark.

Barley Salad

There is nothing like a grain, and barley is a good one. Hot or cold, this adaptable little grain provides a slightly sweet, nutty flavor to recipes.

2½ cups vegetable stock

1¼ cups barley

2 large ripe tomatoes, chopped and seeded

3 scallions, minced

¾ cup mixed chopped red and yellow bell peppers

½ cup minced parsley

2 tablespoons chopped sun-dried tomatoes

¼ cup good-quality extra virgin olive oil

⅓ cup red wine vinegar

salt and freshly ground black pepper

2 tablespoons crumbled feta cheese

washed lettuce leaves for garnish

1. Bring the stock to a boil in a large saucepan. Add barley, cover the pot, and cook over low heat for 30 minutes, until the grain has puffed and absorbed the liquid.

2. Fluff with a fork and cool slightly. Add the tomatoes, scallions, red and yellow peppers, parsley, and sun-dried tomatoes and toss to mix well. Pour the olive oil over the salad and stir to coat. Sprinkle with the vinegar and season with salt and pepper to taste. Arrange the salad in a bowl and sprinkle with cheese.

3. Serve either at room temperature or chilled. Take to the picnic in a covered dish and arrange it on a lettuce-covered plate at the picnic.

Serves 8

Sour Cream Apple Pie

A wonderful alternative to old-fashioned apple pie. It keeps better, too, if there is any left over. Thanks to Irene Maston, a wonderful chef formerly of the Berkshires but now of Andrie Rose Inn in Ludlow, Vermont, for this delightful pie.

---

6 tart baking apples, peeled, cored, and sliced

1½ cups sour cream

½ cup sugar

¼ cup all-purpose flour

1 egg, beaten

pastry for one 9-inch piecrust, unbaked

TOPPING

1 cup chopped walnuts

½ cup (1 stick) butter, melted

½ cup all-purpose flour

⅓ cup firmly packed brown sugar

⅓ cup granulated sugar

1 teaspoon ground cinnamon

1. Preheat oven to 450°F.

2. Place the apples in a large bowl with the sour cream, sugar, flour, and egg. Toss all together until the apples are coated with the mixture.

3. Pour the apple mixture into the piecrust and bake for 10 minutes. Reduce the heat to 350°F and bake for 35 to 40 minutes longer.

4. TO MAKE THE TOPPING, mix the ingredients in a medium-sized bowl. Sprinkle over the pie. Bake 15 to 20 minutes longer, until the topping looks crunchy. Cool the pie on a wire rack and take it to the picnic in the pan.

Makes one 9-inch pie

Autumn Beach Picnic

Menu

Steamed clams

Corn pudding*

Red lettuce salad*

Boiled lobsters
with lemon butter*

Orange slices in Cointreau*
with small biscotti

Hot coffee or red wine

*Recipe included in this chapter

The image of gathering around a roaring beach fire with a kettle of steaming clams and lobsters carefully balanced on the coals is picturesque and inviting. The beach fire, however, may not be allowed, and the cooking results may be problematic. Instead, order the lobsters and clams already cooked from the local seaside fish market. Put them into an old cooler to keep hot while carting them to a secluded spot on the beach.

One such memorable picnic was the day after Thanksgiving on the New Hampshire coast. You may wonder that anyone would want to eat anything other than turkey sandwiches, but we took a deep breath and forced ourselves to enjoy this seafood feast. Parkas and a brisk fire helped keep the cold wind at bay. The lobsters were the best!

Wine Suggestions
Try Beaujolais-Villages from Duboeuf or Louis Jadot.

What Else to Take

For the Food
- An old cooler for the hot seafood
- Mugs for coffee
- Knife for cutting avocado
- Clear plastic cups for dessert

Extras
- Parkas
- Hats
- Gloves

Corn Pudding

*I love corn pudding and could easily embarrass myself by eating the entire dish.
The reward for using fresh corn far exceeds the extra work.*

---

two 10-ounce packages frozen
    corn, thawed and drained,
    or 3 cups fresh corn cut
    from the cob (about 6 ears)
3 eggs, well beaten
¼ cup all-purpose flour
1 tablespoon sugar
½ teaspoon salt
¼ teaspoon freshly ground
    black pepper
  dash ground nutmeg
2 cups milk or light cream
2 tablespoons butter, melted

1. Preheat oven to 325°F. Grease a 1½-quart casserole.

2. In a medium-sized bowl, combine the corn and eggs.

3. Add the flour, sugar, salt, pepper, and nutmeg and mix well. Add the milk and butter and mix again.

4. Pour the pudding mixture into the prepared casserole and bake uncovered for 1 hour 15 minutes, or until set.

5. Cool slightly and store in the refrigerator. Cover the cold pudding carefully for transporting to the beach and serve it at "air" temperature.

Serves 8

Milking the Cob

Fresh corn in summer is as good as it gets. I often cook extra ears and, with a sharp knife, cut off the kernels by holding the cob upright and slicing straight down several rows onto a cutting board. Then, after setting the ear in a bowl, with the back of the knife, I run down the cut rows to milk the cob of all the sweet juices. Store some in freezer bags for making corn pudding in fall.

Red Lettuce Salad

*T*ender curls of red lettuce against vivid green, orange,
and purple is a vision to behold. And it's delicious, too!

---

1 large head red lettuce,
   washed, dried, crisped, and
   torn into small pieces
1 medium purple onion,
   thinly sliced
1 cup drained mandarin
   oranges
1 ripe avocado

LIGHT VINAIGRETTE
3 tablespoons white wine
   vinegar
1 tablespoon lemon juice
1 teaspoon dry mustard
1 teaspoon sugar
¼ teaspoon salt
   freshly ground black pepper
¾ cup vegetable oil

1. Fill a large bowl with lettuce. Wrap the onion and oranges separately and add them to the bowl. Wrap avocado in foil and set it on the lettuce. Cover the bowl and store in the refrigerator until it's time to go.

2. TO MAKE THE LIGHT VINAIGRETTE, place the vinegar, lemon juice, mustard, sugar, salt, and pepper to taste in a blender and mix well. Slowly drizzle in the oil and blend until creamy. Store in a container with a tight-fitting lid and pack in the picnic basket.

3. When at the picnic, assemble the salad. Unwrap the onion and oranges and add to the lettuce. Unwrap and slice the avocado and toss with the lettuce, onion, and oranges. Pour the dressing over the salad, toss again, and serve.

Serves 8

Make individual composed salad plates at home by arranging slices of onion, orange, and avocado on a bed of curly red lettuce. For an added treat, sprinkle with a little crumbled blue cheese or Gorgonzola.

Lemon Butter

*Clarified butter is excellent with lobster, but adding
a bit of lemon and pepper makes it even better.*

½ cup (1 stick) butter, melted
¼ cup lemon juice
¼ teaspoon freshly ground
   black pepper

1. Blend the butter, lemon juice, and pepper and serve warm with the lobsters.

Makes ¾ cup

Clarified Butter

To clarify butter, melt it in a heavy-bottomed saucepan over medium-low heat until bubbly. Skim off the milk solids that rise to the top. For a purer taste, use the clarified butter in this recipe.

Orange Slices in Cointreau

This simple citrus standby is a refreshing finale to an extravagant meal. Transform it to a fancy dessert by serving it in balloon wineglasses.

---

4 large oranges

¼ cup Cointreau or other orange liqueur

8 small biscotti

1. Peel and section the oranges as described on page 98. Pour into a bowl. Add the Cointreau and stir well. Store in a covered bowl until very cold. Serve in clear plastic cups with a biscotti in each one.

Serves 8

Simple, but Special

Fresh fruit embellished with a liqueur or liquor is a simple way to finish a meal. Just slice the fruit and add liqueur. Serve with biscotti or over ice cream, as you wish. Combinations to try: strawberries and crème de cassis; plums and Kirschwasser (cherry brandy); bananas and rum; pears and ginger brandy or Poire William; apples and Calvados; or peaches and peach brandy.

Teddy Bear's Birthday Party Picnic

Menu

Baked chicken fingers
with dipping sauces*

———

Skinny sticks*

———

Banana frosty*

———

Teddy bear cookies*
and ice cream

*Recipe included in this chapter

An old rule of thumb was that the number of children at a birthday party should equal the age of the birthday child. This party for preschoolers breaks that rule and provides for a party of six to eight three- or four-year-olds.

To create a picnic atmosphere, even if the party is indoors, give each child a medium-sized brown bag, preferably with handles. As an early party activity, let them decorate their bags with teddy bear stickers and their own artwork. Put lunch bags with plastic utensils, a plastic bag of chicken fingers, and a plastic bag of skinny sticks in these brown bags and place them on the table, so each child knows where to sit. Save the larger bags for the party favors that each child will take home. Serve the frosties in small plastic cups and serve the cookies at the end with ice cream.

What Else to Take

For the Food

- Small bowls for dipping sauces
- Lunch bags for food

Extras

- Plastic tablecloth for indoors or outdoors
- Medium-sized brown bags with handles
- Assorted teddy bear stickers, crayons, and markers for decorating the bags

- A little teddy bear for each child to take home as a party favor
- A large teddy bear for a centerpiece
- Balloons, streamers, and party games/activities

Baked Chicken Fingers
with Dipping Sauces

Kids love these little morsels. They are easy to eat and
not filled with fat as in fast-food places.

1½ pounds chicken tenders
1 egg
1 cup coarse bread crumbs
¼ teaspoon freshly ground
   black pepper
¼ teaspoon salt
¼ teaspoon dried thyme
 dash of cayenne pepper
   (optional and probably best
   saved for teenagers)

DIPPING SAUCES
1 cup cocktail sauce
1 cup honey combined with 1
 tablespoon Dijon mustard
 for honey mustard sauce
1 cup plum sauce

1. Preheat oven to 350°F. Spray a jelly-roll pan with vegetable cooking spray.

2. Rinse and pat dry the chicken. Cut each tender into pieces about 1½ inches long.

3. In a pie pan, beat the egg. In another pie pan, mix the bread crumbs and seasonings. Dip pieces of chicken into the egg and then roll in bread crumbs.

4. Arrange the chicken on the prepared pan.

5. Bake for 15 minutes, until the chicken is lightly browned and cooked through. Cool slightly and store in the refrigerator. When chilled, pack 3 or 4 pieces in 8 resealable plastic bags to put into each child's lunch bag.

6. Put the sauces in shallow bowls and have enough so that the children don't have to reach to dip.

Serves 8 preschoolers

Skinny Sticks

Tender, crunchy, and sweet, these healthy veggies are fun to eat!

---

3 carrots
2 red bell peppers

1. Peel the carrots and cut into julienne strips. Steam the carrots over boiling water for 1 to 2 minutes until tender crisp. Wash the pepper and cut into julienne strips. Toss them together and store covered in the refrigerator.

2. Before the party, make up resealable plastic bags of carrots and peppers; put into each child's lunch bag.

8 servings

Banana Frosty

Frosties are delicious, creamy, ice cold, and bursting with fruit flavor.

---

1 banana, peeled and thickly sliced
1½ cups orange juice
1 cup plain yogurt
2 tablespoons sugar
dash of cinnamon

1. Place all of the ingredients in a blender container and blend at high speed until frothy. Serve immediately.

Each recipe makes 8 small servings

Note: To make strawberry frosties, use 2 cups frozen unsweetened strawberries or washed and hulled fresh ones; ¾ cup milk; ¾ cup plain yogurt; and ¼ cup sugar.

Teddy Bear Cookies

USE THE RECIPE FOR STRAWBERRY COOKIES ON PAGE 107 FOR MAKING THE BATTER.

Use teddy bear cookie cutters of different sizes and bake as directed. Decorate with a simple icing and colorful sprinkles. This is a great project for involving your preschooler. The child can help make the dough. It's best if you set out all the decorating supplies and do the piping. But a preschooler can help ice the cookies, put on currant eyes, and do a fantastic job with sprinkles. The kitchen floor will be a mess, but the cookies will be wonderful.

————————————

ICING

4 *cups confectioners' sugar*

3 to 4 *tablespoon lemon juice*

food coloring

assorted colorful sprinkles, currants for decorating

plastic bag with a tiny corner cut off for piping, or cake decorating set

1. TO MAKE THE ICING, mix the sugar and lemon juice in a small bowl until smooth. Divide into smaller bowls and add desired food coloring.

2. For piping, add a little more sugar to make a thicker icing and spoon it into a plastic bag. Snip a small hole in one corner. Squeeze the bag from the top and twist as icing comes out. Enlarge the hole, if needed.

1 cup

Wine-Country Picnic

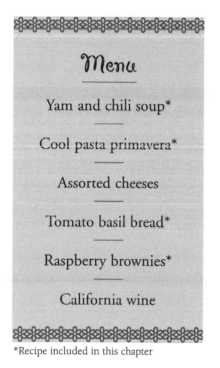

What Else to Take

- Serrated knife and cutting board
- Soup cups and spoons
- Swiss Army knife

A loaf of bread, a glass of wine, plus fabulous soup, salad, and dessert, are the ingredients for an outstanding wine country picnic. Our favorite way to do this is to wander through Napa Valley or Sonoma County with leisurely stops at vineyards to sample their treasures, and eventually find a winery with picnic tables looking out at a fabulous view of vine-clad hillsides. The vineyards of California are the oldest and most well-known in the United States, but as interest in wines has grown and wine-making techniques have improved, wineries have become more prevalent throughout the country.

A simpler picnic approach than taking homemade food is stopping at a wonderful food store and selecting your soup, salad, bread, cheese, and dessert from its displays. In either case, remember the designated driver and have a great time.

Wine Suggestions

Eric Murray of the Oakville Grocery, Joseph Phelps Vineyards, recommends Gewurztraminer: "The spicy, floral character of the wine is a perfect foil for the spices, while the slight sweetness is cooling, similar to a chutney served with curry" or Saintsbury's Garnet, "A light-bodied engagingly fruity pinot noir perfectly suited to picnic fare."

Yam and Chili Soup

The unusual combination of flavors makes this tasty soup a vintage California dish and a wonderful surprise to the palate. A favorite store in California wine country, the Oakville Grocery, gave me this memorable recipe.

CRÈME FRAÎCHE
- 1 cup heavy cream
- 1 cup sour cream

SOUP
- ½ cup butter
- 1 large onion, thinly sliced
- 4 cloves of garlic, crushed
- 1 to 2 cayenne chiles, seeded
- ¼ teaspoon ground cumin
- 2½ pounds yams, peeled and sliced
- 6 cups chicken stock
- salt

GARNISHES
- ½ cup scallions, cut on bias
- ¼ cup chopped fresh cilantro
- 1 cup crème fraîche (plain yogurt may be substituted)

1. TO MAKE THE CRÈME FRAÎCHE: mix the heavy cream and sour cream and let sit at room temperature for 24 hours.

2. TO MAKE THE SOUP, melt the butter in a large pot. Sauté the onion and garlic with the chiles and cumin until the onions are soft. Add the yams and cook over low heat until the onions are golden and the yams are slightly coated, about 10 to 15 minutes.

3. Add the chicken stock, bring to a boil, and simmer for 15 minutes, until the yams are soft when pierced with a fork. Salt to taste.

4. Purée the soup in a food processor, and then pass it through a sieve. Pack it in a thermos bottle until picnic time.

5. Garnish each serving with the scallions, cilantro, and a swirl of crème fraîche.

Serves 8

Yams and Sweet Potatoes

True yams grow only in Asia and Africa. For us, the terms sweet potato *and* yam *are interchangeable and refer to those orange-fleshed, highly nutritious tubers from the morning glory family that are unrelated to white potatoes. Sweet potatoes can be kept in a cool, dry place for up to a month.*

Cool Pasta Primavera

Another interesting twist on an old theme from the Oakville Grocery.
The garlic cream sauce is a nice change from vinaigrette.

1 pound tricolor rotelle
   pasta, cooked al dente
   and drained

1 small bunch broccoli, cut
   into bite-size pieces and
   lightly blanched

½ pound cauliflower, cut
   into bite-size pieces and
   lightly blanched

¾ cup red bell peppers, cut
   into 2-inch julienne strips
   (yellow or green bell
   pepper optional for
   additional color)

¾ cup zucchini, cut into
   quarters lengthwise, then
   into ¼-inch slices

½ cup cherry tomatoes

GARLIC CREAM SAUCE

1 to 2 cloves of garlic, crushed

1 tablespoon lemon juice

¼ teaspoon salt

½ cup olive oil

¼ cup heavy cream

1. Combine the pasta and vegetables in a large bowl.

2. TO MAKE THE CREAM SAUCE, mix the garlic, lemon juice, and salt in a food processor. With the machine running, slowly add the oil until the mixture is thick. Blend in the heavy cream and pour over the pasta and vegetables. Chill for at least 1 hour.

Serves 8 to 10

Heightened Taste

To heighten and set the color and flavor of the vegetables, blanch them in a steamer basket in a saucepan or a pot filled with a steamer insert. Bring about 1 inch of water to a boil and place vegetables in the steamer. Place the steamer in the pan, cover and steam for 1 to 2 minutes until the color brightens and the vegetables are slightly tender.

Tomato Basil Bread

The aroma and flavor of this colorful bread, originally from the Alexis Baking Company in Napa Valley, are reminiscent of pizza.

---

2 tablespoons olive oil
½ cup chopped onions
2 cloves of garlic, minced
1 tablespoon active dry yeast
2 cups warm (110°F) water
¾ cup tomato purée
4 cups unbleached all-purpose flour
1 tablespoon dried basil
2 teaspoons salt
½ teaspoon sugar

1. In a medium-sized saucepan, heat the oil and sauté the onions for about 10 minutes, until soft. Add the garlic at the end of the cooking time. Let cool.

2. In a large bowl, dissolve the yeast in the water. Add the tomato purée and mix.

3. In a medium-sized bowl, combine the dry ingredients and add to the yeast mixture. Add the onions, garlic, and oil and mix well.

4. Turn the dough out onto a floured surface and knead until the dough is smooth and elastic. Return the dough to the bowl and cover with a damp cloth. Let it rise until doubled in size, about 1 hour 30 minutes.

5. Grease a baking sheet. Punch down the dough and shape into a round free-form loaf and place on the baking sheet. Let it rise slightly while the oven is preheating.

6. Preheat oven to 400°F.

7. Bake for 35 to 40 minutes, or until it is lightly browned and sounds hollow when tapped. Remove the loaf from the baking sheet and cool completely on a wire rack.

8. Either slice the loaf in advance or take a cutting board and a bread knife to the picnic. To transport it to the picnic, put the loaf into a plastic bag and place in a bread basket, lined with a colorful napkin.

Makes 1 loaf

Raspberry Brownies

A dense, rich chocolate and a hint of raspberries combine to make a chocolate lover's dream come true. Another fabulous creation from the Alexis Baking Company, this is by far my favorite brownie recipe. And besides that, you make it in one pot.

8 *ounces unsalted butter*

4 *ounces unsweetened chocolate*

2 *cups sugar*

1 *teaspoon salt*

1 *teaspoon vanilla extract*

4 *eggs*

1 *cup unbleached all-purpose flour*

2 *cups walnut pieces*

1 *scant cup raspberry preserves*

I cut these brownies into about 1-inch squares, because they are so rich.

1. Grease a 9- by 13-inch baking pan.

2. Melt the butter and chocolate in a large, heavy saucepan over low heat, stirring occasionally.

3. Remove the pan from the heat and add the sugar, salt, and vanilla and mix well. Add the eggs, one at a time, mixing after each addition. Add the flour and beat until smooth. Stir in the walnut pieces.

4. Pour *half* the batter into the prepared pan and make a smooth surface. Freeze the batter for 30 minutes.

5. Preheat oven to 350°F.

6. When the batter is frozen, spread the preserves on top in a thin layer. Pour the remaining batter over the preserves and gently smooth it over to cover the preserves.

7. Bake for 40 to 45 minutes, or until a tester inserted in the center comes out clean.

8. Cool the pan on a wire rack for 10 minutes before cutting the brownies. Cool the brownies completely on the wire rack.

9. Place the brownies on a pretty plate, cover them with plastic wrap, and pack in the picnic basket.

Makes 16 brownies

WINTER
WANDERINGS

Winter is the cozy season when our thoughts turn to hearty soups and stews, long cold nights, firelight, and frosty air. For most, picnicking outdoors has little appeal, but skiing, snowboarding, or snowshoeing brings color to many cheeks and sparkle to many eyes. Winter picnics are designed for those who want to snuggle by a warm fire, and also those who venture out in search of vigorous activity before warming themselves with food by the fireside.

Picnics

- Cross-Country Ski Picnic
- "Baby, It's Cold Outside" Picnic
- Après-Ski Picnic
- Workday Picnic

Cross-Country Ski Picnic

Menu

Multibean soup*

———

Thinly sliced roast beef
and saga blue cheese

———

Caretaker Farm bread*

———

Kate and Meg's chocolate
chip oatmeal cookies*

———

Thirst-quenching oranges

———

Chai-inspired spiced tea*

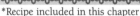

*Recipe included in this chapter

On cold, sunny winter days, the sky against the white snow seems bluer than at any other time of year. Woods filled with soft snow, intricate lace patterns of trees cut against the deep blue sky, frosty breath and rosy cheeks, and we're enjoying a day of cross-country skiing. The experience is intense and the appetites grow large. Hot, hearty food is the perfect antidote to the cold, crisp air that quickly wraps around the steaming bodies of the skiers as they stop for a quick lunch.

What Else to Take

For the Food
- Thermos bottles for the soup
- Insulated bags to keep the beef, cheese, and oranges from freezing
- Cold water to supplement the oranges

Extras
- Day packs
- Space blanket for the lunch stop

Multibean Soup

*This soup is an all-time favorite in our family. We double the recipe
and freeze the excess for a quick dinner on a cold night.*

¼ cup each dried red kidney
  beans, green split peas,
  yellow split peas, lentils,
  black-eyed peas, navy
  beans, lima beans, black
  turtle beans, and pinto
  beans (can be bought
  already mixed in a 1-
  pound bag).
2 tablespoons barley
2 quarts water
1 to 2 pounds kielbasa, cut into
  1-inch chunks
2 cloves of garlic, minced
1 bay leaf
1 28-ounce can tomato
  purée
1 medium onion, chopped
2 tablespoons lemon juice
1 tablespoon chili powder
1 teaspoon dried savory
½ teaspoon dried thyme
½ teaspoon salt
  freshly ground black pepper

1. Wash the beans and barley thoroughly. In a soup pot, cover them with water and soak them overnight. In the morning, drain off the water and put the beans and barley back into the pot. Add the 2 quarts of water, kielbasa, garlic, and bay leaf. Bring to a boil over high heat, and then simmer gently for 2½ to 3 hours, stirring occasionally.

2. Add the remaining ingredients and simmer for 30 minutes longer. Remove the bay leaf and pour into wide-mouthed thermos bottles.

Serves 8

For thoughtful hostess or holiday gifts, mix a huge batch of the dried beans, pack into pretty bottles, and tie on a card with the recipe.

Caretaker Farm Bread

Elizabeth sells this delicious, healthful bread, warm from the farmhouse bakery, to go with the beautiful organic produce fresh from the fields at Caretaker Farm.

---

1 cup old-fashioned rolled oats

2 cups hot water

2 tablespoons active dry yeast

½ cup warm (110°F) water

¼ cup honey

3½ cups unbleached all-purpose flour

2 cups whole-wheat flour

¼ cup vegetable oil

1 teaspoon salt

½ cup raisins (optional)

¼ cup sunflower seeds (optional)

Baking bread seems very time-consuming, when, in fact, much of the time allows for the dough to rise. But, it can rise quickly by the stove or slowly in the refrigerator to suit your schedule.

1. Mix the oats in the hot water and let the mixture stand for 30 minutes.

2. Dissolve the yeast in the warm water in a large bowl. Add the honey and 2 cups of the all-purpose flour and beat vigorously with a wooden spoon for several minutes. Stir the oats into the flour mixture and let sit for 30 minutes.

3. Add the remaining all-purpose flour and beat well. Add half of the whole-wheat flour, the oil, and salt and beat some more. Add the remaining whole-wheat flour, raisins, and sunflower seeds and beat well. When it's difficult to beat the dough with a spoon, place it on a floured surface for kneading.

4. Knead the dough for 10 minutes. Put the dough into a clean, oiled bowl. Turn the dough over to coat it with oil, cover it with a damp cloth, and let the dough rise in a draft-free place until it is double in size, 45 minutes to 1 hour.

5. Grease two 9- by 5-inch loaf pans. Punch down the dough and return it to the floured work surface. Divide the dough in half and shape each half into a loaf. Place the loaves into the prepared pans. Let the loaves rise for 1 hour, or until they mound slightly above the tops of the pans.

6. Preheat oven to 400°F.

7. Bake the loaves for 30 to 40 minutes, or until golden brown and hollow sounding when tapped with your knuckles. When cool, slice the bread and make sandwiches.

Makes 2 loaves

Kate and Meg's Chocolate Chip Oatmeal Cookies

My daughters, Kate and Meg, perfected a basic chocolate chip cookie recipe with this fabulous result. Meg made hundreds of dozens to sell at a local deli during the summers when she was in college.

2¼ cups all-purpose flour

1 teaspoon baking soda

½ teaspoon salt

¾ cup firmly packed brown sugar

½ cup granulated sugar

½ cup (1 stick) unsalted butter, softened and cut into 1-inch chunks

½ cup (1 stick) margarine, softened and cut into 1-inch chunks

2 eggs

1 teaspoon vanilla extract

1½ cups old-fashioned rolled oats

1½ cups chocolate chips

1. Preheat oven to 350°F.

2. Mix the flour, baking soda, and salt in a large bowl.

3. In the large bowl of an electric mixer, mix the sugars at low speed. Add the chunks of butter and margarine and continue to beat at low speed, then increase to high speed and beat until light and fluffy. Add the eggs and vanilla at low speed, then increase to high speed.

4. At low speed, add the flour mixture ½ cup at a time, then increase to high speed until the mixture is well blended. Stir in the oats and chocolate chips with a wooden spoon.

5. Drop rounded tablespoonfuls onto an ungreased baking sheet and bake for 10 minutes, or until golden brown. Remove the cookies from the oven and cool on wire racks for a minute or two before removing them from the baking sheet. Cool cookies completely on wire racks and pack in a resealable plastic bag for traveling in the picnic pack.

Makes 3½ dozen cookies

Chai-Inspired Spiced Tea

Imagine a dreary, cold, rainy weekend, a great book, a comfy chair, and a steaming mug of this spicy mix, which is wonderfully warming for picnics.

---

6 *tablespoons tea, or 6 tea bags*

3 *whole cloves*

2 *whole cardamom pods, cracked*

1 *stick cinnamon*

1 *tablespoon honey*

6 *cups boiling water*

1 *cup scalded milk*

1. Place the tea, cloves, cardamom, cinnamon, and honey in a large teapot. Pour the boiling water over the tea and let sit for at least 5 minutes. Add the milk and stir well.

2. Strain the tea into two 1-quart thermos bottles and pack in the packs.

Serves 8

Why Chai?

Chai *is Russian and Swahili for "tea." In coffee shops, chai is a concoction made with black tea, spices, sugar, and steamed milk — a hot, frothy, highly satisfying drink. It also can be frosted by placing it in a blender with ice cubes for a cool spicy mix.*

"Baby, It's Cold Outside" Picnic

Menu

Baked brie with fresh fruit*

Mustardy pork loin
with fruit conserve*

Broccoli salad with
Caesar dressing*

Roasted rosemary
potatoes and onions*

Crusty bread

Panna cotta
with raspberry sauce*

*Recipe included in this chapter

For some picnics, the hearth is the best location, whether it's at home or in a cozy lodge in the mountains. As in all the other picnics, you prepare the food ahead and take it to the picnic spot. Even though you move only from the kitchen to the fireside, for this romantic evening picnic for two, arrange the food on pretty plates and bowls and pack it all in a basket to take to the hearth. Set a low table by the fire, open the wine, light the candles, and be ready for romance.

What Else to Take

- Tablecloth and napkins
- Candles
- Wineglasses
- A vase with a single rose

Baked Brie
with Fresh Fruit

*Irene Maston shared this elegant recipe with me.
I could eat it every day, but try to reserve it for festive occasions.*

⅔ of a 1-pound package
phyllo dough

⅓ cup butter, melted

1 pound brie, cut into four
wedges

apple wedges

grapes

strawberries

*For a little crunch, add
sliced almonds to the top
of the brie before covering
it with phyllo.*

1. Unroll the phyllo sheets and keep them covered with plastic wrap to prevent them from drying out. Remove two sheets of phyllo and brush the top one with butter.

2. Lay a wedge of the brie diagonally on the phyllo sheet, about two inches from one corner. Fold the phyllo over the cheese and continue to roll the brie up in the phyllo sheet. Fold the ends in when half of the phyllo is used up. Finish rolling until the whole sheet is used up and the brie is neatly packaged. Repeat the process until all the brie is used up. Chill the brie for 30 minutes. The recipe can be made to this point, covered tightly with plastic wrap, and stored in the refrigerator for a day.

3. Preheat oven to 400°F.

4. On a baking sheet, bake the phyllo for 10 to 12 minutes, or until golden brown.

5. Gently remove the brie from the baking sheet after it has cooled slightly, and set it on a pretty plate. Arrange the fruit around it.

Makes 4 wedge-shaped appetizers

Mustardy Pork Loin
with Fruit Conserve

A simple pork loin becomes elegant when flavored with mustard and combined with this lush fruit conserve. Another of Irene's masterpieces.

---

3 to 4 pounds boneless pork loin

3 cloves of garlic, minced

½ to ¾ cup coarse mustard
freshly ground black pepper
several fresh rosemary sprigs

FRUIT CONSERVE

1 pound plums, peaches, or nectarines, pitted and chopped

1½ cups sugar

¾ cup raisins

¼ cup water

1 tablespoon grated orange zest

¼ cup orange juice

¼ cup chopped walnuts

1. Preheat oven to 375°F.

2. Place the loin on a rack in a shallow roasting pan. Spread the outside with the garlic and cover with a thick layer of the mustard. Sprinkle with the pepper and rosemary.

3. Bake for 30 to 35 minutes per pound, or to 160°F internal temperature. Remove the meat from the pan and chill. Slice enough meat for two and store the leftovers in the refrigerator for sandwiches or another meal. Arrange slices on a platter and cover lightly with aluminum foil until ready to serve.

4. TO MAKE THE FRUIT CONSERVE, combine the fruit, sugar, raisins, water, and zest in a large, heavy saucepan. Bring the mixture to a boil and simmer for 20 minutes.

5. Add the orange juice and simmer for 10 minutes longer. Add the walnuts and simmer an additional 5 minutes. Remove the conserve from the heat, cool slightly, and chill. Put the conserve into a dish with a tight-fitting cover to pack in the picnic basket. Serve conserve alongside the slices of pork.

Serves 8

Broccoli Salad
with Caesar Dressing

As colorful as it is tasty, this salad, also from Irene, always adds a touch of class.

---

3 cups broccoli florets, with
   2-inch stems
½ medium red onion, thinly
   sliced
½ medium red bell pepper,
   seeded and thinly sliced
¼ cup sliced black olives
4 romaine leaves

DRESSING
¼ cup grated Parmesan
   cheese
3 anchovy fillets
2 parsley sprigs
2 teaspoons minced garlic
2 teaspoons Dijon mustard
1 teaspoon capers
freshly ground black pepper
1 cup olive oil
2 tablespoons lemon juice
¼ cup red wine vinegar

1. Fill a bowl with ice water. Blanch the broccoli in boiling water for 1 minute, or until bright green. Plunge immediately into the ice water. Drain, place in a bowl, and toss with the onion, pepper, and olives.

2. Wash romaine leaves, wrap in paper towels, and store in a plastic bag in the refrigerator.

3. TO MAKE THE DRESSING, blend the Parmesan, anchovies, parsley, garlic, mustard, capers, and pepper to taste in a food processor. Slowly drizzle in the oil. Add the lemon juice and vinegar. Pour over the broccoli and chill until ready to serve.

Serves 4

Roasted Rosemary Potatoes and Onions

Rosemary perfumes the caramelized potatoes and onions with scents from the forest in this dish that is so simple and so sensational you won't believe it.

¾ pound new potatoes, red or white, or a combination

1 medium onion

1 tablespoon olive oil

1 tablespoon chopped fresh rosemary

salt and freshly ground black pepper

1. Preheat oven to 450°F.

2. Wash and scrub the potatoes and cut into wedges. Dry with paper towels to remove excess moisture. Peel the onion, remove ends, and cut into wedges. Toss the potatoes and onions with the oil and rosemary in a large bowl and pour into a large roasting pan.

3. Spread the potatoes and onions in a single layer and roast for 30 minutes, stirring occasionally. When the potatoes are tender and lightly browned, remove from oven, season to taste with salt and pepper, and pour into a serving dish. Cover lightly with aluminum foil until ready to serve.

Serves 2

Panna Cotta
with Raspberry Sauce

*This divinely simple alternative to baked custard or
Bavarian cream I ate almost daily when I lived in Florence.
It is a regular on Tuscan menus and means, simply, cooked cream.*

PANNA COTTA

- 1 *package unflavored gelatin*
- 4 *teaspoons cold water*
- 2 *cups heavy cream or half-and-half*
- ¼ *cup sugar*
- 1 *teaspoon vanilla extract*

RASPBERRY SAUCE

- 1 *cup fresh or frozen raspberries*
- 2 *tablespoons sugar*
- 1 *tablespoon Kirschwasser or other fruit brandy or cassis (optional)*

If the thought of heavy cream or half-and-half does not appeal to you, substitute milk for at least half of it.

1. TO MAKE THE PANNA COTTA, soften the gelatin in the water until dissolved.

2. While the gelatin softens, heat the cream and sugar over low heat until the sugar dissolves and the cream is warm, stirring often.

3. Remove from heat, add the gelatin and stir until it melts. Stir in the vanilla and pour into individual wine goblets. Let cool until set and serve with a drop of syrupy, aged balsamic vinegar; fresh berries; or raspberry sauce. Cover the surface of the remaining two with plastic wrap and store in the refrigerator.

4. TO MAKE THE RASPBERRY SAUCE, process ½ cup of the raspberries, the sugar, and Kirschwasser in a food processor or blender for 10 seconds, or until smooth. Pour into a bowl and stir in the remaining raspberries.

Serves 4 (makes 1 cup of raspberry sauce)

Après-Ski Picnic

Menu

Spicy beans with sausage*

Green beans and tomatoes*

Mexican corn bread*

Brownies*

Hot chocolate or Glüwein*

*Recipe included in this chapter

After a day on the slopes, try an indoor picnic by the fire in a ski lodge or cabin or condo. Spread the food on a low table, take off those heavy ski boots, relax, and enjoy good food and fellowship. Being warm and cozy inside feels even better as the temperature drops and the wind howls outside.

What Else to Take

- Mugs
- Cozy socks and slippers
- Sweatpants and soft shoes
- CD player and CDs
- Candles

Spicy Beans with Sausage

This hearty dish, which requires time but not much labor in the kitchen, will warm those skiers through and through. It is a great "make ahead" dish.

---

2 cups dried navy beans, soaked overnight, rinsed, and drained

1 cup dried red kidney beans, soaked overnight, rinsed, and drained, or substitute 6 cups canned beans for 3 cups dried

1 bay leaf

6 cups water

1 tablespoon corn oil

1 medium onion, chopped

1 clove of garlic, minced

one 10-ounce package frozen corn

5 slices bacon, crisp-cooked, drained, and crumbled

1 medium green bell pepper, seeded and chopped

2 tablespoons tomato paste

1 tablespoon brown sugar

1 tablespoon white wine vinegar

1 teaspoon chili powder

½ teaspoon salt

freshly ground black pepper

1 to 2 pounds kielbasa, cut into 1-inch chunks

½ cup grated Cheddar cheese

1. Cover the navy and kidney beans and bay leaf with the water in a large pot. Bring to a boil over high heat, then turn the heat down and simmer for 1 hour, or until the beans are tender. Drain the beans and reserve the liquid.

2. Preheat oven to 250°F.

3. Transfer the beans and 3 cups of the reserved liquid to a Dutch oven and bake, covered tightly, for 8 hours, stirring occasionally. Add more liquid if beans begin to dry out.

4. While the beans are baking, heat the oil in a medium-sized skillet and sauté the onion and garlic for 2 minutes, until slightly softened.

5. Remove the beans from the oven. Turn up the oven to 350°F.

6. Add to the beans the onion, garlic, corn, bacon, pepper, tomato paste, sugar, vinegar, chili powder, salt, and pepper to taste.

7. Cook the kielbasa in a skillet for about 15 minutes and add it to the beans. Stir to mix and return the beans to the oven for 30 to 40 minutes, or until bubbly. Just before serving, sprinkle the Cheddar. This casserole can be frozen and thawed en route to the ski area and gently reheated.

Serves 8

Green Beans and Tomatoes

A dish that adapts to the seasons. Use good-quality canned tomatoes for best results. My favorite is San Marzano from Italy.

---

2 pounds fresh green beans, trimmed and cut into 2-inch pieces, or two 10-ounce packages frozen green beans

½ cup olive oil

2 large onions, thinly sliced

4 cloves of garlic, minced

1½ teaspoons dried basil

¼ cup minced fresh parsley

salt and freshly ground black pepper

one 28-ounce can tomatoes, drained of all but ½ cup juice, or, 3½ cups chopped tomatoes

1. Preheat oven to 350°F.

2. Fill a large saucepan half full of water and bring it to a boil. Parboil the beans for 2 or 3 minutes. Or partially cook the frozen beans according to the directions on the package. Drain the beans and place in a 2-quart shallow casserole.

3. In a medium-sized skillet, heat the oil over medium heat and sauté the onions and garlic until soft.

4. Add the basil, parsley, salt and pepper to taste, and tomatoes with juice to the onion mixture and mix well. Spoon the onion mixture over the beans. Bake for 20 minutes. Cool the beans completely, cover with plastic wrap, and refrigerate for a day before serving. These beans can be made ahead and served at room temperature.

Serves 8

Mexican Corn Bread

This lively corn bread based on a recipe from The Moosewood Cookbook *by Mollie Katzen (1977) is made especially for those who love texture and crunch and lots of flavor.*

---

1 cup yellow cornmeal
1 cup all-purpose flour
1 tablespoon baking powder
½ teaspoon salt
1 cup milk
1 egg, lightly beaten
1 tablespoon honey
¼ cup olive oil
1 medium onion, minced
1 cup fresh or frozen whole kernel corn
½ cup grated Cheddar cheese

1. Preheat oven to 375°F and grease an 8-inch square baking pan.

2. In a large bowl, combine the cornmeal, flour, baking powder, and salt.

3. In a small bowl, beat together the milk, the egg, and the honey.

4. Heat the oil in a small skillet. Add the onion and sauté over medium heat for 5 minutes, or until soft.

5. Add the egg mixture to the flour mixture, and mix thoroughly. Add the corn, Cheddar, and onion mixture, and mix well.

6. Spread the batter in the prepared pan. Bake for 25 to 30 minutes, or until brown and firm on top. Cool the bread in the pan on a wire rack. When cool, cut into squares.

**Makes one 8-inch-square pan
(to serve 8 generously, make two)**

To crank up the heat, use pepper jack cheese instead of Cheddar, or add some chopped jalapeño peppers to the batter.

Brownies

Don't kid yourself that these are healthful. They are just plain good and very rich with a dense chocolate flavor. To have some leftovers and to allow for snitching, double the recipe.

1½ cups sugar

½ cup (1 stick) butter, softened

3 eggs

3 ounces unsweetened chocolate, melted

½ cup all-purpose flour

½ teaspoon baking powder

½ teaspoon salt

¾ cup semisweet chocolate chips

¾ cup chopped pecans or walnuts (optional)

1 teaspoon almond extract

1. Preheat oven to 350°F and grease a 9-inch square baking pan.

2. In a medium-sized bowl, cream the sugar and butter together until fluffy. Beat in the eggs, one at a time. Add the melted chocolate and beat well.

3. In a small bowl, sift together the flour, baking powder, and salt. Add the flour mixture to the chocolate mixture and stir to blend. Add the chocolate chips, nuts, and almond extract and and mix well.

4. Pour the batter into the prepared pan. Bake for 35 to 45 minutes, or until a tester inserted in the center comes out clean. Cool in the pan on a wire rack. When cool, cut into squares, cover pan with foil, and bring with you. Serve on a plate.

Makes one 9-inch-square pan

Glüwein
(Hot Spiced Wine)

This fruity, spicy mulled wine that was a staple of our holiday parties for years is a German festive favorite.

---

one 1.5-liter bottle burgundy
     wine
  2 lemons, sliced
  2 oranges, sliced
  5 whole cloves
  3 whole allspice berries
  3 cinnamon sticks

1. Place all of the ingredients in a heavy kettle. Gently heat the mixture, but do not let it boil. A woodstove is the perfect place to keep this spiced wine hot.

Serves 8

Glüwein is relatively low in alcohol. A similar drink with more kick, one to beware of, is Swedish glogg, made with the same flavorings but mixed with brandy or aquavit instead of red wine.

Workday Picnic

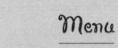

Menu

Broccoli soup

Great sandwiches*

Asian vegetable salad*

Prize-winning chocolate chip
cookies* and Anjou pears

Flavored seltzer waters

*Recipe included in this chapter

unches that we take to work can be boring. Busy people are apt to take lunch on the run, at their desks, or, in some cases, to skip it altogether. Treat yourself and be good to your body by taking some time for lunch and eating a substantial one. Having a good lunch and, incidentally, also a good breakfast, carries you through a long workday and prevents the late-afternoon munchies. To simplify, skip the sandwiches and add grilled chicken strips to the vegetable salad to make it heartier.

What Else to Take

- Plants or a bouquet of flowers
- A bright tablecloth
- Sunshine
- Colorful paper plates and plastic utensils

Great Sandwiches

One way to have great sandwiches is to buy them from a bakery or food shop. An alternative is to gather interesting breads, cheeses, meats, and vegetables and arrange them in baskets and on platters so people can build their own. This approach will satisfy the grazing instincts that many of us have.

Building a Great Sandwich

You can build a sandwich however you wish. What's your favorite combination? If you don't have one, try these:

• **Vollkornbrot** *spread with goat cheese and topped with cucumbers and onions*

• *Focaccia topped with Asiago, roasted red bell peppers and salami*

• *Thick slices of country bread spread with saga blue and topped with ham*

• *Turkey and avocado slices sandwiched between slices of sourdough bread*

Fixings for Great Sandwiches

Essentials	Suggestions
Breads	Olive bread, crusty country *bâtarde,* sourdough baguette, focaccia, German whole-grain bread, or *Vollkornbrot*
Cheeses	Goat cheese, Italian Asiago, sharp Cheddar, saga blue, smoked Gouda
Meats	Thin slices Italian hard salami, peppercorn turkey breast, Danish ham
Vegetables	Paper-thin cucumber slices, transparent onion rings, roasted red bell peppers, avocado slices
Condiments	Assorted mustards, mayonnaise

Asian Vegetable Salad

This recipe was recommended by the folks at the Oakville Grocery in California. A pungent Asian vinaigrette coats these crisp fresh vegetables for a lovely, light salad.

---

1 large bunch broccoli, cut into florets and diagonal stalks, lightly blanched

1 cup carrots, cut in half, thinly sliced on bias

1 cup celery, cut on bias

1 cup chopped fresh cilantro

1 cup drained pickled baby corn

½ pound fresh green beans, lightly blanched

6 scallions, cut on bias

2 small red bell peppers, cut into julienne strips

4 ounces shiitake mushrooms, stems removed, quartered, and blanched

2 ounces fresh-water chestnuts, blanched

DRESSING

½ cup peanut oil

¼ cup sesame oil

¼ cup soy sauce

3 cloves of garlic, finely chopped

3 tablespoons black sesame seeds

2 tablespoons plum sauce

2 tablespoons rice wine vinegar

1- to 2-inch regular piece ginger root, peeled and grated

1. Combine all of the vegetables (blanched† if desired) in a large bowl.

2. TO MAKE THE DRESSING, whisk together the ingredients in a small bowl.

3. Pour the dressing over the prepared vegetables and toss well. Cover and chill for 1 hour before packing for the picnic.

Serves 8

†See box on page 151 for blanching instructions.

XXXXXXXXXXXXXXXXXXXX

Cut the vegetables in small bite-size pieces so knives won't be necessary. Strive to make them all about the same size.

Prize-Winning Chocolate Chip Cookies

*These rich, moist, double chocolate chip cookies, from
101 Perfect Chocolate Chip Cookies (Storey Books, 2000), won the
grand prize in a national search for the perfect chocolate chip cookie conducted
by an inn in Williamstown, Massachusetts. A cookie-lover's dream!*

1¾ cups all-purpose flour

¼ teaspoon baking soda

1 cup (2 sticks) butter, softened

1 teaspoon vanilla extract

1 cup granulated sugar

½ cup firmly packed brown sugar

1 egg

⅓ cup unsweetened cocoa

2 tablespoons milk

1 cup semisweet chocolate chips

1 cup chopped pecans or walnuts

1. Preheat oven to 350°F. Line baking sheet with foil (not necessary if using nonstick pans).

2. Combine the flour and baking soda in a medium-sized bowl and set aside.

3. In the large bowl of an electric mixer, cream the butter at high speed. Add the vanilla and sugars and beat until fluffy. Beat in the egg. At low speed, beat in the cocoa, then the milk.

4. With a wooden spoon, stir in the flour mixture and mix until just blended. Add the chocolate chips and nuts and stir to combine.

5. Drop the dough by rounded teaspoonfuls onto the baking sheets. Bake for 12 to 13 minutes, or until set. Remove the cookies from the oven and cool on wire racks for 2 minutes before removing them from the baking sheet. Cool cookies completely on wire racks and pack them in a brown bag to take to the picnic.

Makes 3 dozen

Metric Conversion Charts

Unless you have finely calibrated measuring equipment, conversions between U.S. and metric measurements will be somewhat inexact. It's important to convert the measurements for all of the ingredients in a recipe to maintain the same proportions as the original.

GENERAL FORMULA FOR METRIC CONVERSION

Ounces to grams	multiply ounces by 28.35
Grams to ounces	multiply grams by 0.035
Pounds to grams	multiply pounds by 453.5
Pounds to kilograms	multiply pounds by 0.45
Cups to liters	multiply cups by 0.24
Fahrenheit to Celsius	subtract 32 from Fahrenheit temperature, multiply by 5, then divide by 9
Celsius to Fahrenheit	multiply Celsius temperature by 9, divide by 5, then add 32

APPROXIMATE METRIC EQUIVALENTS BY VOLUME

U.S.	METRIC
1 teaspoon	5 millileters
1 tablespoon	15 millileters
¼ cup	60 milliliters
½ cup	120 milliliters
1 cup	230 milliliters
1¼ cups	300 milliliters
1½ cups	360 milliliters
2 cups	460 milliliters
2½ cups	600 milliliters
3 cups	700 milliliters
4 cups (1 quart)	0.95 liter
1.06 quarts	1 liter
4 quarts (1 gallon)	3.8 liters

APPROXIMATE METRIC EQUIVALENTS BY WEIGHT

U.S.	METRIC	METRIC	U.S.
¼ ounce	7 grams	1 gram	0.035 ounce
½ ounce	14 grams	50 grams	1.75 ounces
1 ounce	28 grams	100 grams	3.5 ounces
1¼ ounces	35 grams	250 grams	8.75 ounces
1½ ounces	40 grams	500 grams	1.1 pounds
2½ ounces	70 grams	1 kilogram	2.2 pounds
4 ounces	112 grams		
5 ounces	140 grams		
8 ounces	228 grams		
10 ounces	280 grams		
15 ounces	425 grams		
16 ounces	454 grams		
(1 pound)			

Index

Other Storey Titles You Will Enjoy

101 Perfect Chocolate Chip Cookies, by Gwen Steege. Whether you like your chocolate chip cookies with or without nuts, chewy or crumbly, traditional, exotic, healthy, adventurous, decadent, or completely over-the-top, you'll find the perfect recipe in *101 Perfect Chocolate Chip Cookies.* 144 pages. Paperback. ISBN 1-58017-312-8.

The Healthy College Cookbook, by Alexandra Nimetz, Jason Stanley & Emeline Starr. Created by and for college students. More than 200 healthy, tasty, cheap, and easy-to-make recipes — many for the vegetarian — will see even the most hapless cooks through those demanding college years. 160 pages. Paperback. ISBN 1-58017-126-5.

Apple Cookbook, by Olwen Woodier. This book features unusual recipes that use North America's favorite fruit in beverages, appetizers, snacks, brunches, entrées, and desserts. 160 pages. Paperback. ISBN 1-58017-389-6.

500 Treasured Country Recipes from Martha Storey and Friends, by Martha Storey. In this chock-full-of-recipes cookbook, Martha shares her family's and friends' favorite tried-and-true country-cooking recipes. These are the simple dishes with country style that make your mouth water. 544 pages. Paperback. ISBN 1-58017-291-1.